Alone

Words and Music by Billy Steinberg and Tom Kelly

4

Gtr. 2: w/ Rhy. Fig. 3, 2 times

I nev-er real-ly cared un-til I met you. And now it chills me to the bone.

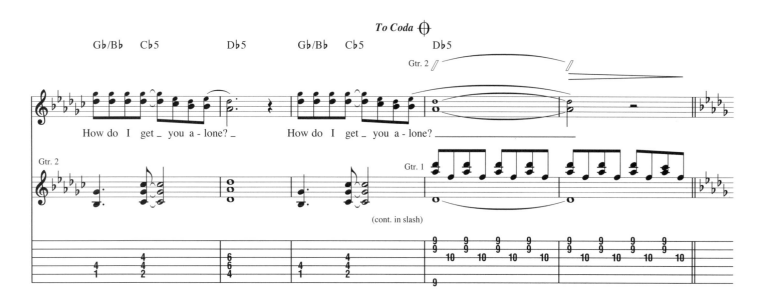

To Coda ✛

How do I get _ you a-lone? _ How do I get _ you a-lone?

(cont. in slash)

Verse

Gtr. 1: w/ Rhy. Fig. 1, 2 times
Gtr. 2 tacet

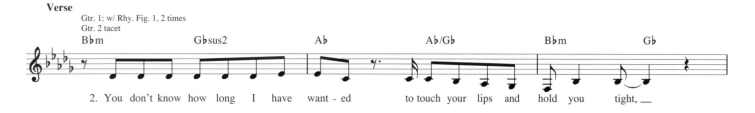

2. You don't know how long I have want-ed to touch your lips and hold you tight, _

oh. _ You don't know how long I have wait-ed, and I was gon-na

Gtr. 1: w/ Rhy. Fig. 2

tell you to-night. _ But the se-cret is still _ my own, _____ and _ my

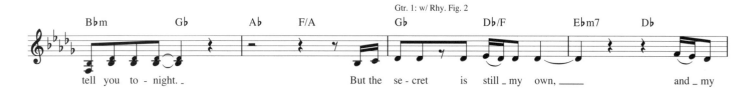

love for you _ is still un - known. _ A - lone.

Pre-Chorus

Gtr. 2: w/ Rhy. Fig. 3, 2 times
Gtr. 1 tacet

D.S. al Coda

Oh, ___ oh, ___ whoa. ___

⊕ *Coda*

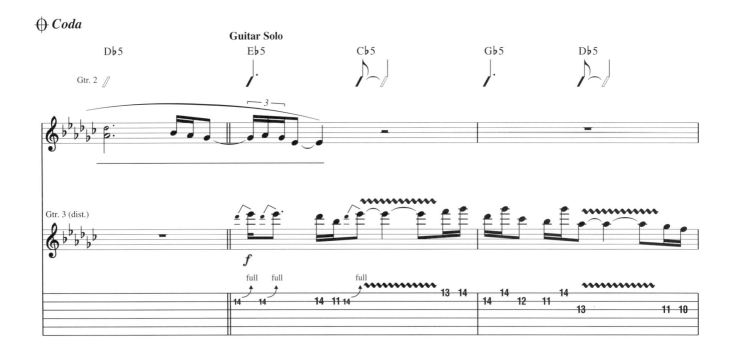

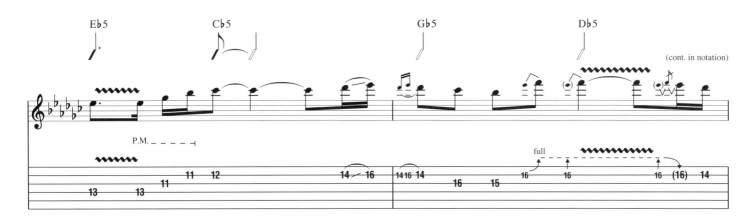

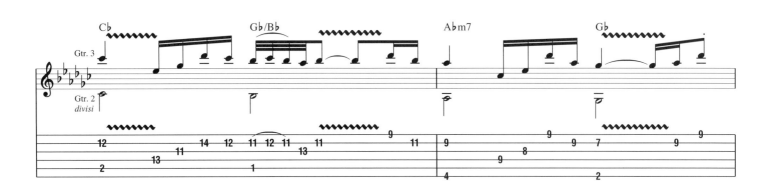

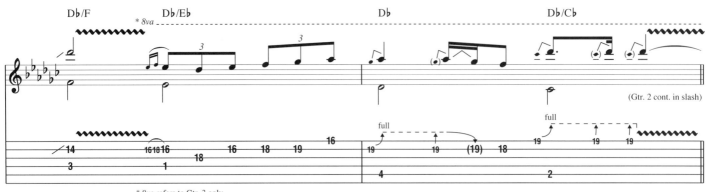

* 8va refers to Gtr. 3 only.

Any Way You Want It

Words and Music by Steve Perry and Neal Schon

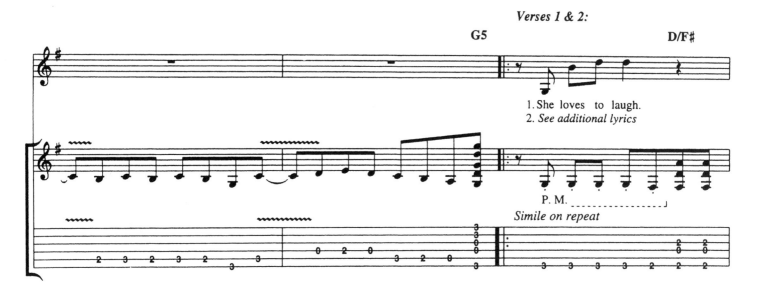

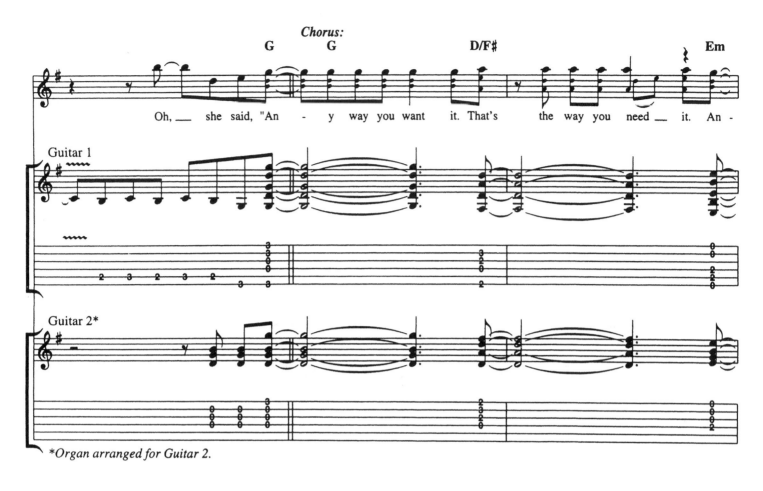

*Organ arranged for Guitar 2.

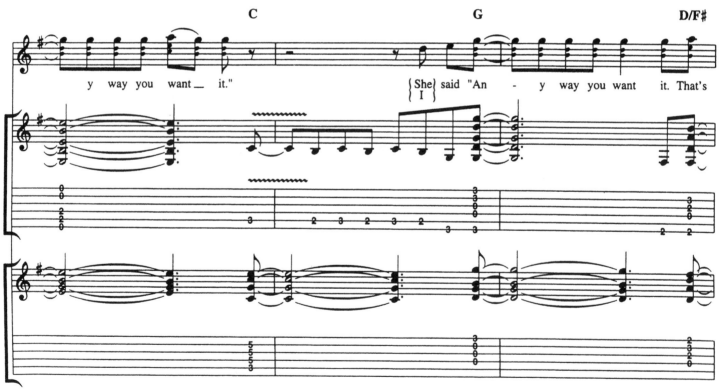

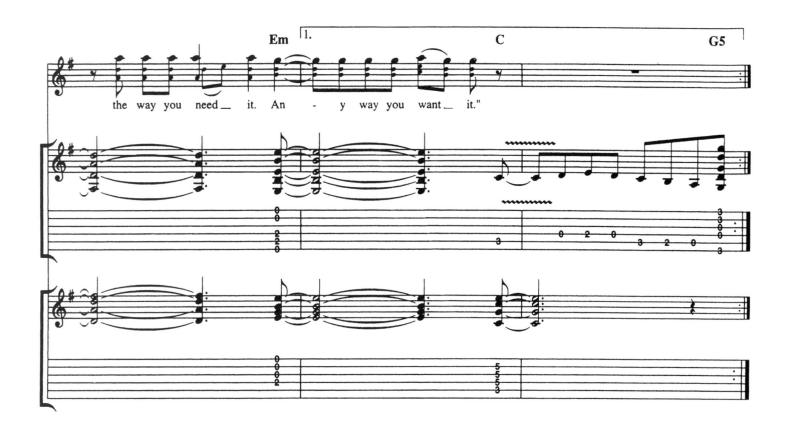

the way you need it. An - y way you want it."

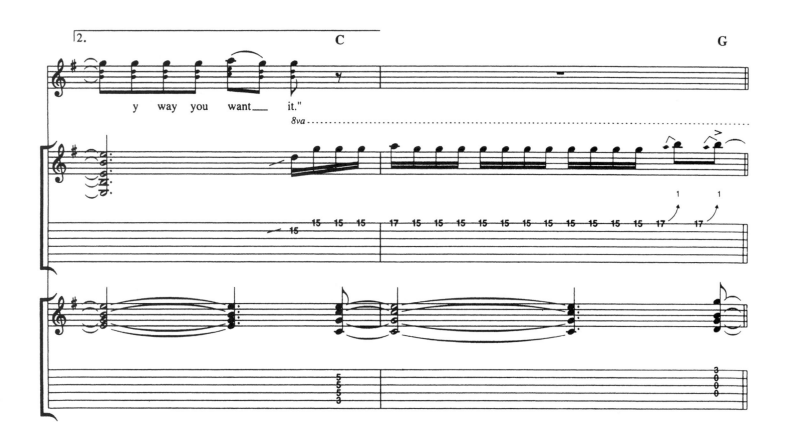

y way you want it."

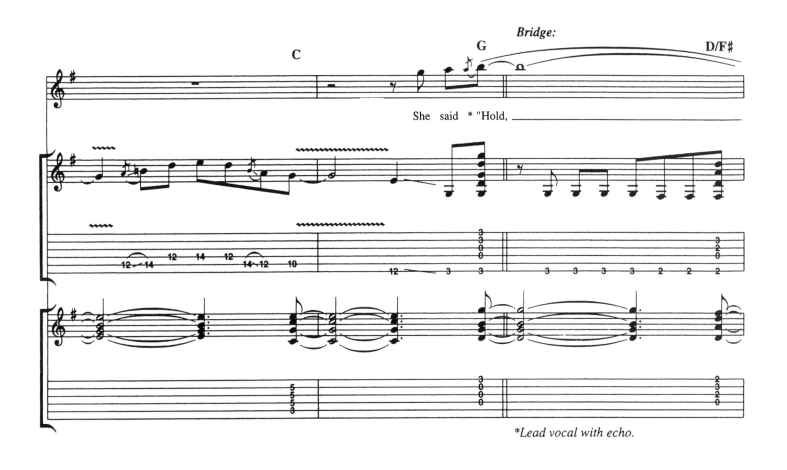

She said * "Hold,

*Lead vocal with echo.

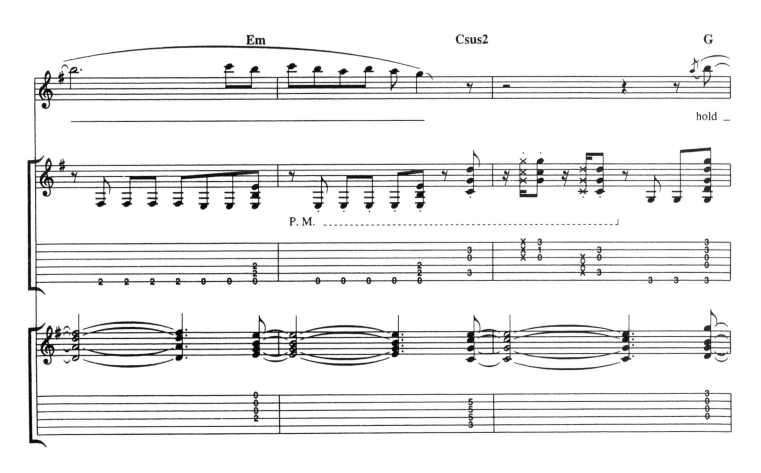

hold

P. M.

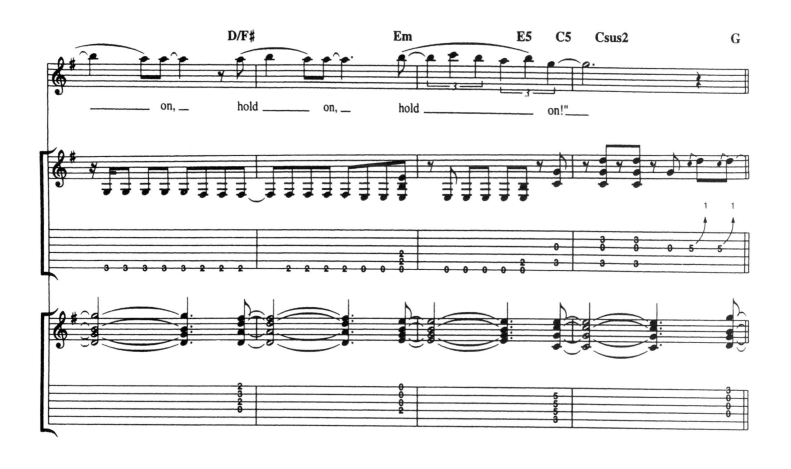

on, _____ hold _____ on, _ hold _____ on!"

Guitar Interlude:

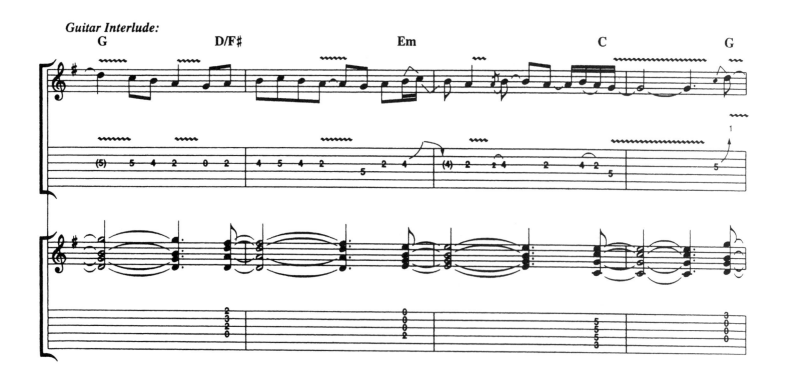

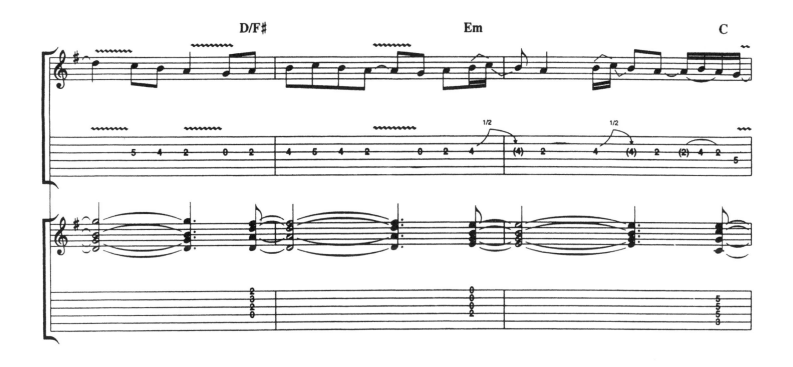

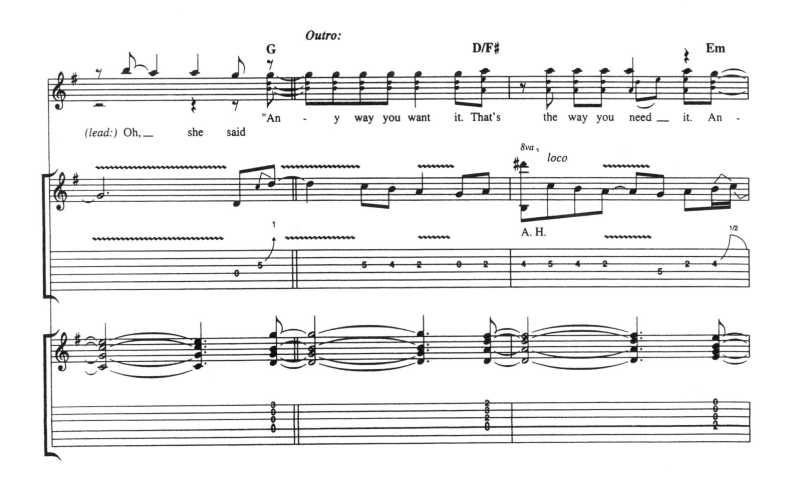

(lead:) Oh,— she said

"An - y way you want it. That's the way you need — it. An -

G   D/F♯   Em

y way you want it. That's the way you need __ it. An -

C   G

y way you want __ it. An -

Let ring

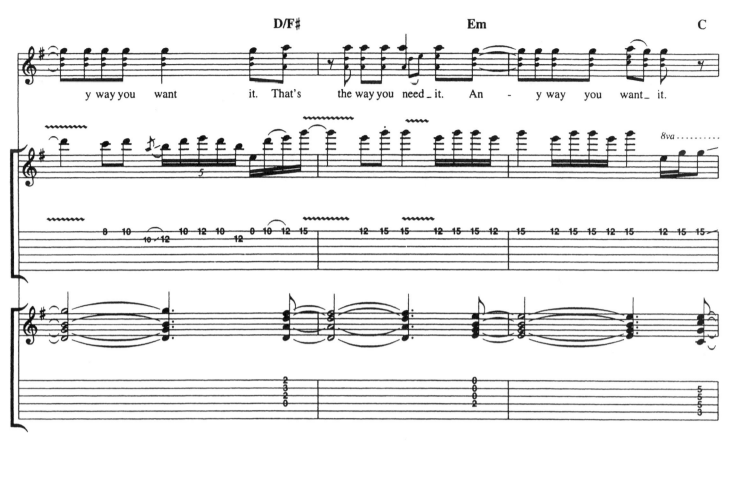

y way you want it. That's the way you need it. An - y way you want it.

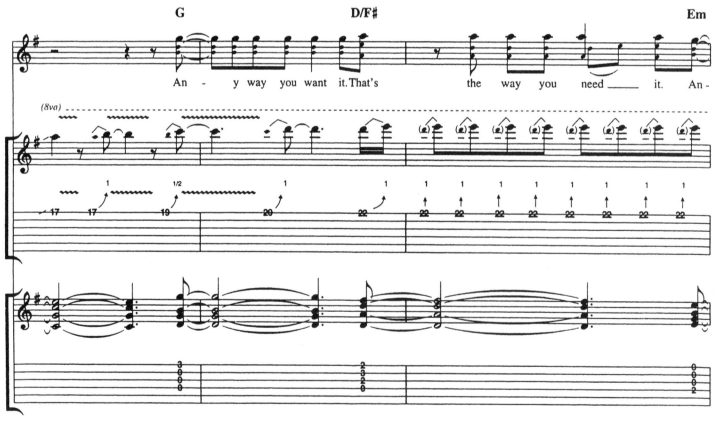

An - y way you want it. That's the way you need it. An -

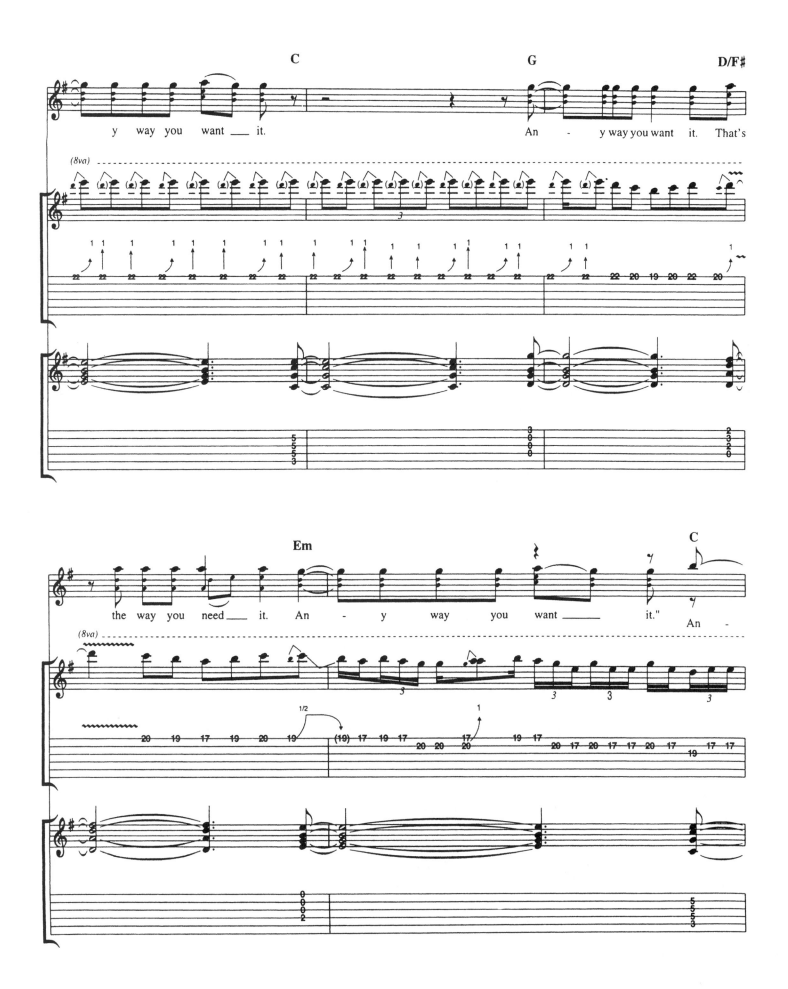

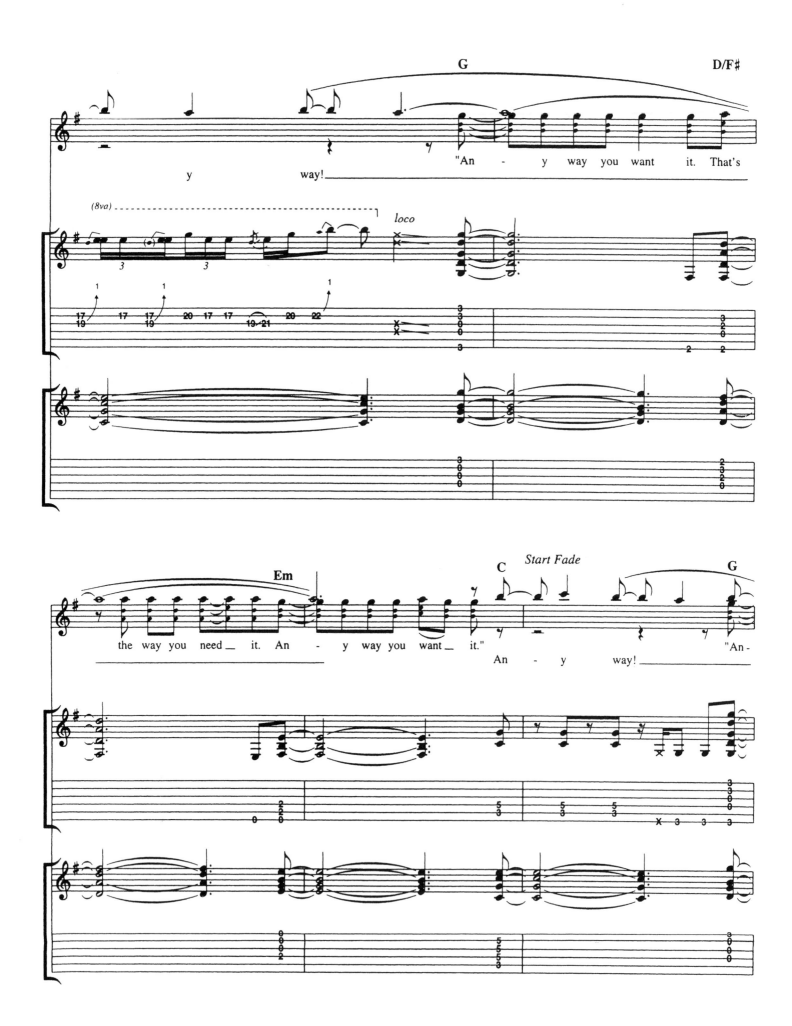

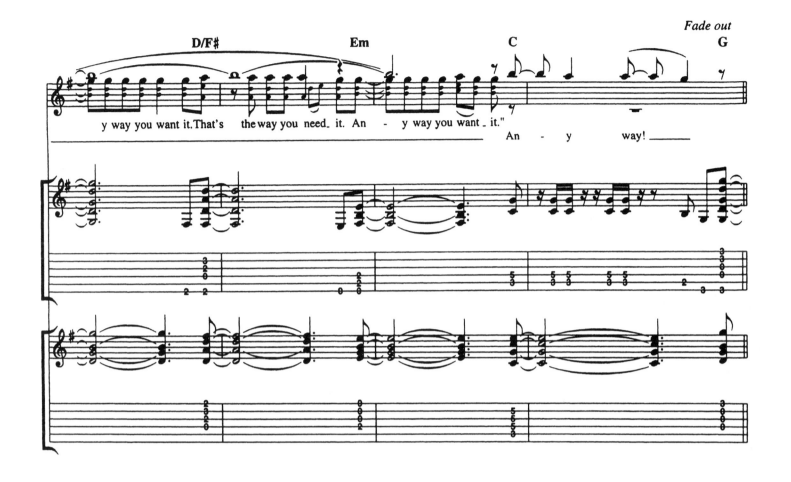

Additional Lyrics

Verse 2: I was alone,
I never knew
What good love can do.
Ooh, then we touched,
Then we sang,
About the lovin' things.

Ooh, all night, all night,
Oh, every night.
So hold tight, hold tight,
Oh, baby, hold tight.
(To chorus)

Beth

Words and Music by Bob Ezrin, Stanley Penridge and Peter Criss

Intro

Moderately ♩ = 117

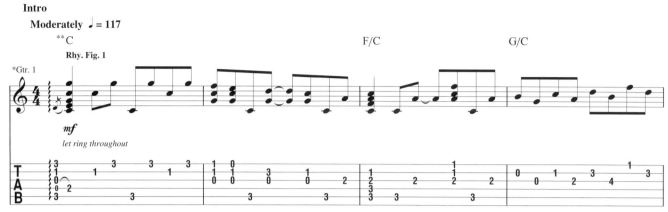

*Composite of piano & orchestra arr. for gtr.

**Chord symbols reflect basic harmony.

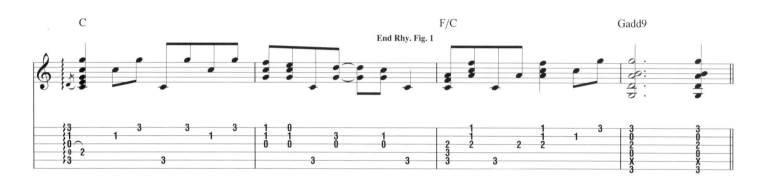

Verse

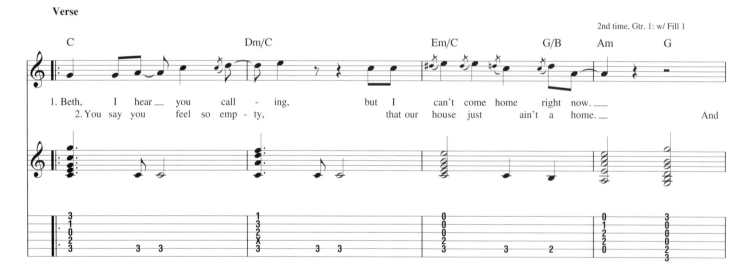

1. Beth, I hear you call - ing, but I can't come home right now.

2. You say you feel so emp - ty, that our house just ain't a home. And

Fill 1

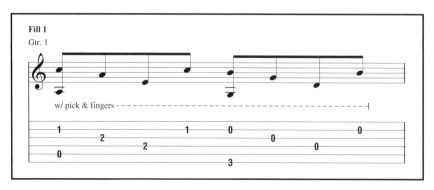

w/ pick & fingers

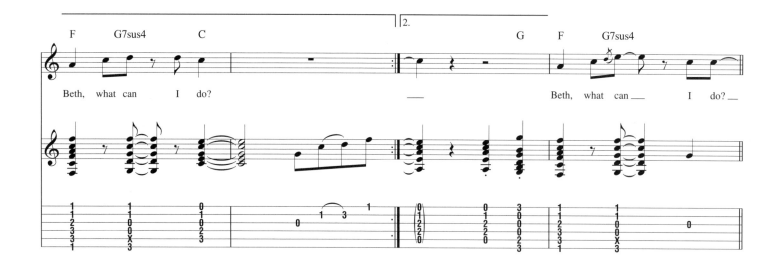

Beth, what can I do? Beth, what can I do?

Interlude

Gtr. 1: w/ Rhy. Fig. 1

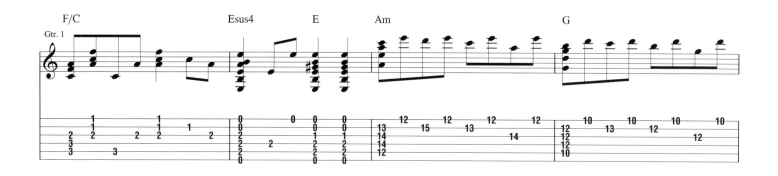

Gtr. 1

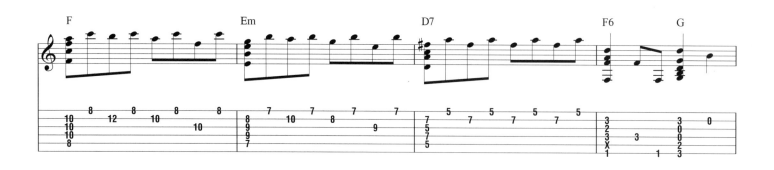

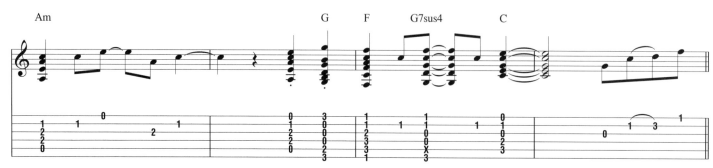

Verse

3. Beth, I know __ you're lone - ly and I ____ hope you'll __ be al - right, __

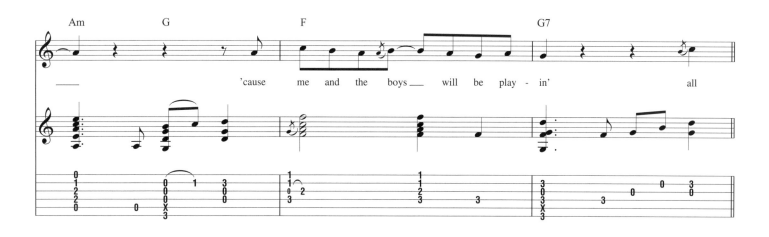

'cause me and the boys __ will be play - in' all

Outro

Gtr. 1: w/ Rhy. Fig. 1

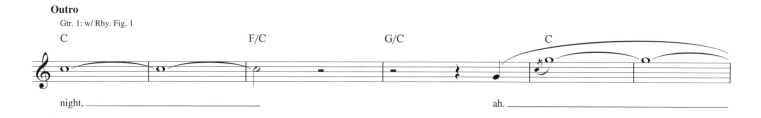

night, _____ ah.

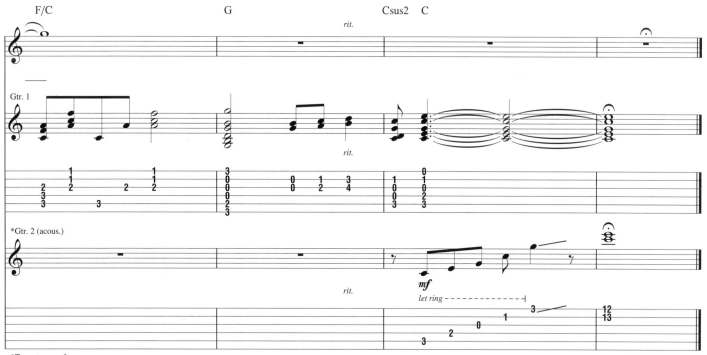

*Two gtrs. arr. for one.

Bohemian Rhapsody

Words and Music by Freddie Mercury

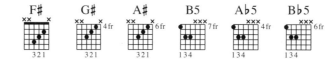

I don't want to die, ___
(Ooh. _____)
(Ooh, ___

I some-times wish I'd nev-er been born at all. ___
ooh, ___ ooh, ___ ooh. ___)

Guitar Solo

(Ooh. _____ Ooh.)

Rhy. Fig. 2

End Rhy. Fig. 2

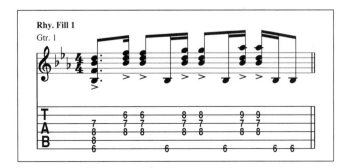

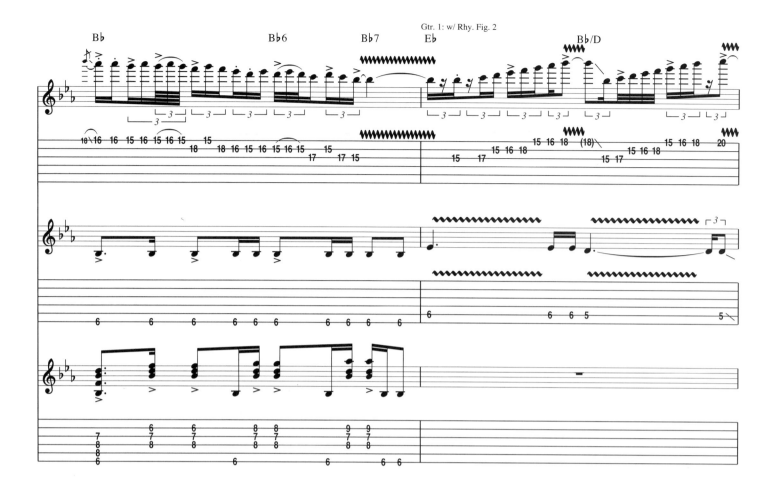

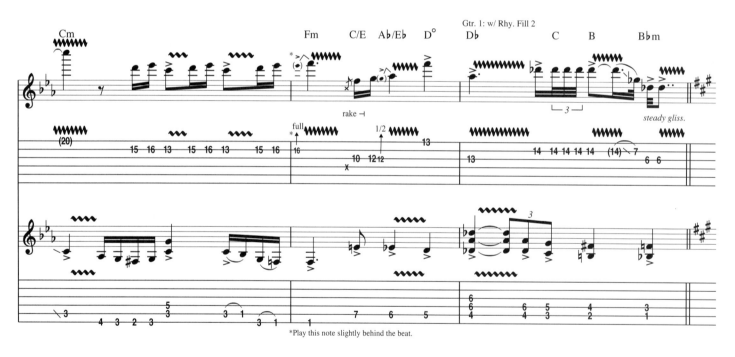

*Play this note slightly behind the beat.

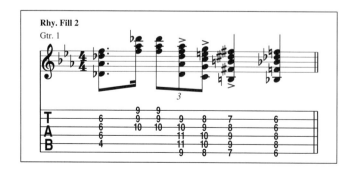

*Each of these notes is sung by a separate voice,
and each sustains into the next meas.

*Separate voices; sustain all notes.

32

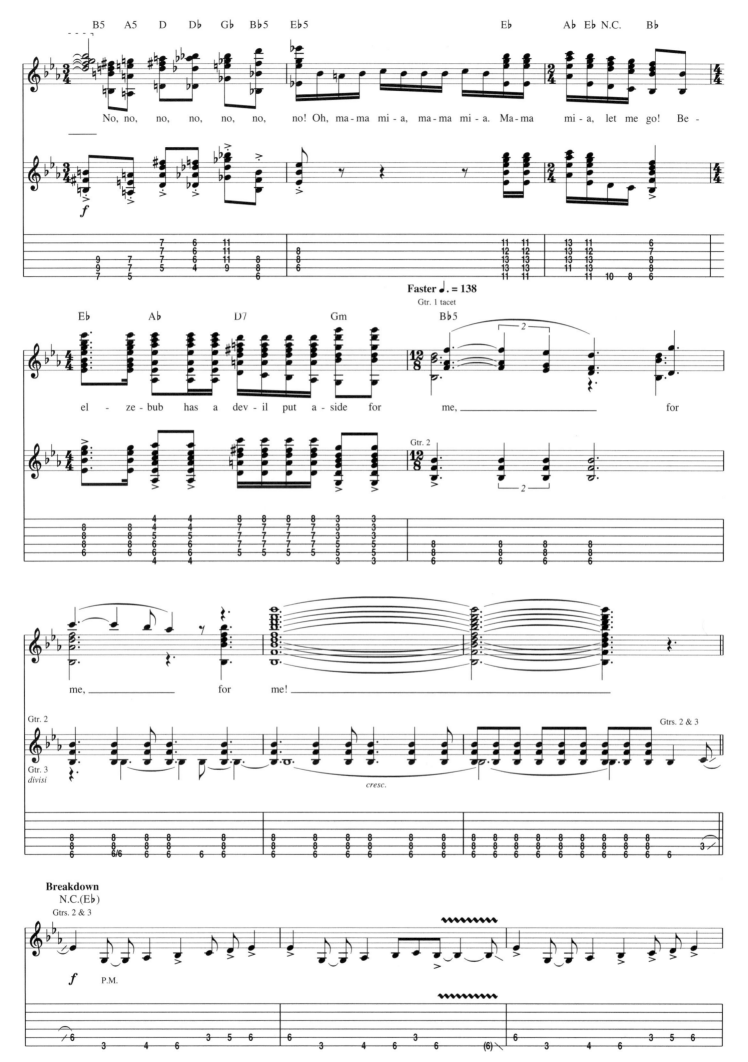

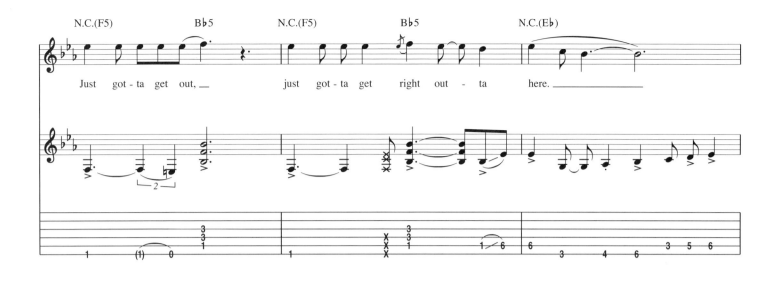

Just got-ta get out, ___ just got-ta get right out-a here. ___

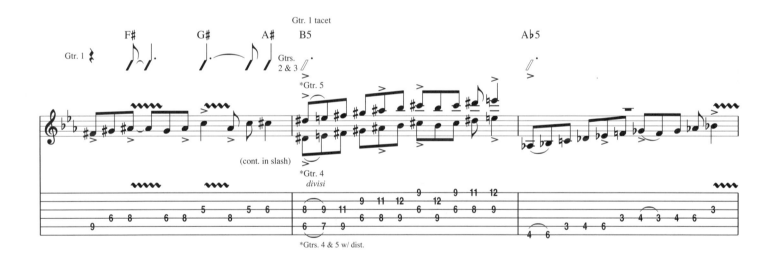

*Gtrs. 4 & 5 w/ dist.

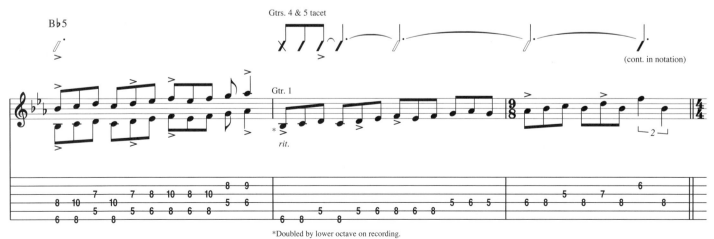

*Doubled by lower octave on recording.

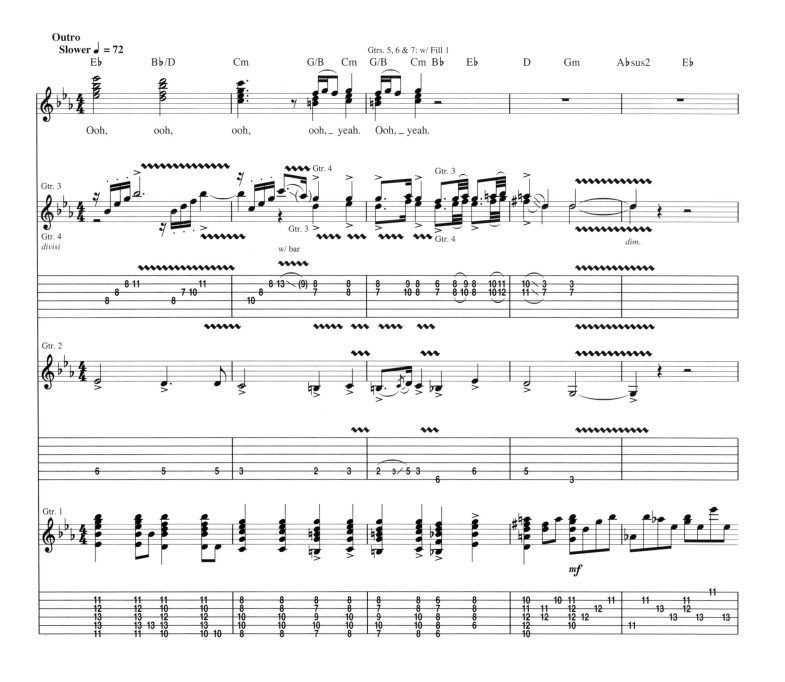

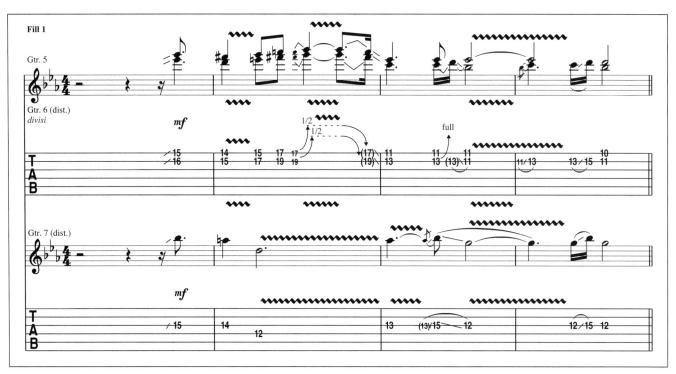

Bust a Move

Words and Music by Marvin Young and Matt Dike

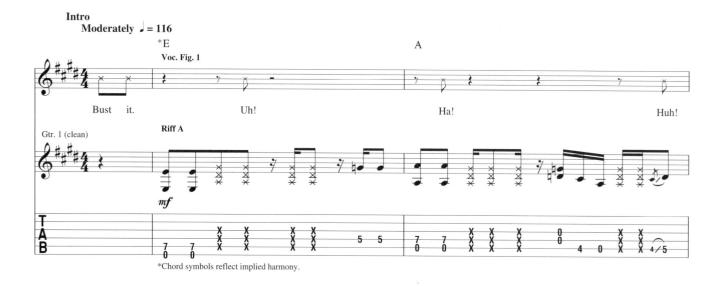

Bust it.   Uh!   Ha!   Huh!

*Chord symbols reflect implied harmony.

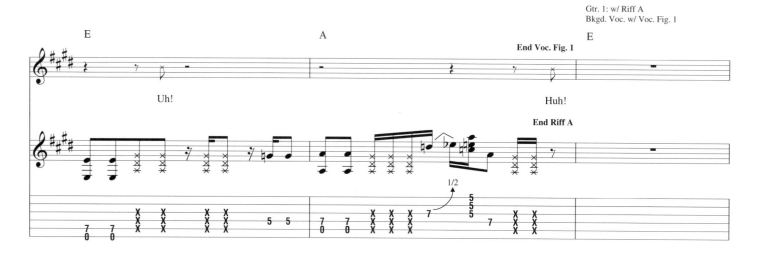

Uh!   Huh!

1. This __

Verse

Gtr. 1: w/ Riff A (1 1/2 times)
Bkgd. Voc.: w/ Voc. Fig. 1 (1 3/4 times)

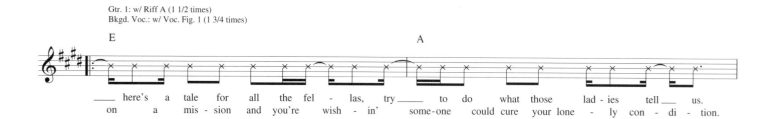

__ here's a tale for all the fel - las, try __ to do what those lad - ies tell __ us.
on a mis - sion and you're wish - in' some-one could cure your lone - ly con - di - tion.

Get shot down 'cause you're o - ver zeal - ous, play __ hard to get, fe - males get jeal - ous.
Look - in' for love in all __ the wrong pla - ces, no fine girls just ug - ly fac - es.

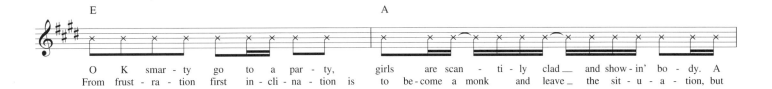

O K smar - ty go to a par - ty, girls are scan - ti - ly clad __ and show - in' bo - dy. A
From frus - tra - tion first in - cli - na - tion is to be - come a monk and leave __ the sit - u - a - tion, but

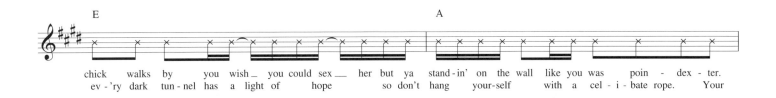

chick walks by you wish __ you could sex __ her but ya stand - in' on the wall like you was poin - dex - ter.
ev - 'ry dark tun - nel has a light of hope so don't hang your - self with a cel - i - bate rope. Your

2nd time, Gtr. 2: w/ Rhy. Fill 1

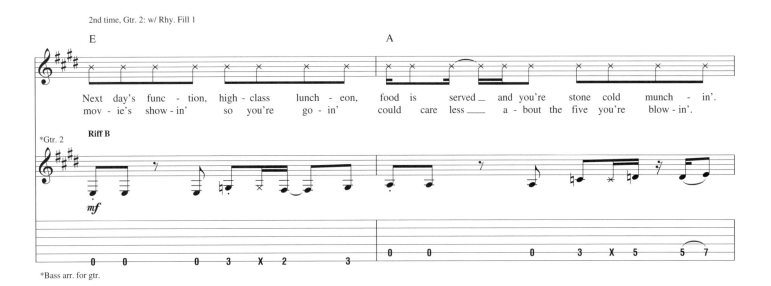

Next day's func - tion, high - class lunch - eon, food is served __ and you're stone cold munch - in'.
mov - ie's show - in' so you're go - in' could care less __ a - bout the five you're blow - in'.

Riff B

*Gtr. 2

mf

*Bass arr. for gtr.

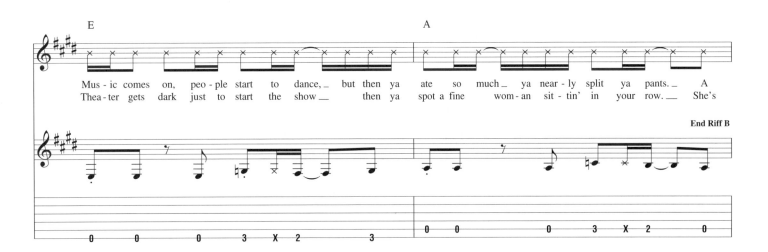

Mus - ic comes on, peo - ple start to dance, but then ya ate so much __ ya near - ly split ya pants. __ A
Thea - ter gets dark just to start the show __ then ya spot a fine wom - an sit - tin' in your row. __ She's

End Riff B

Rhy. Fill 1

Gtr. 2

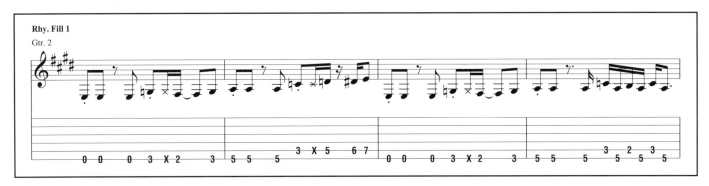

39

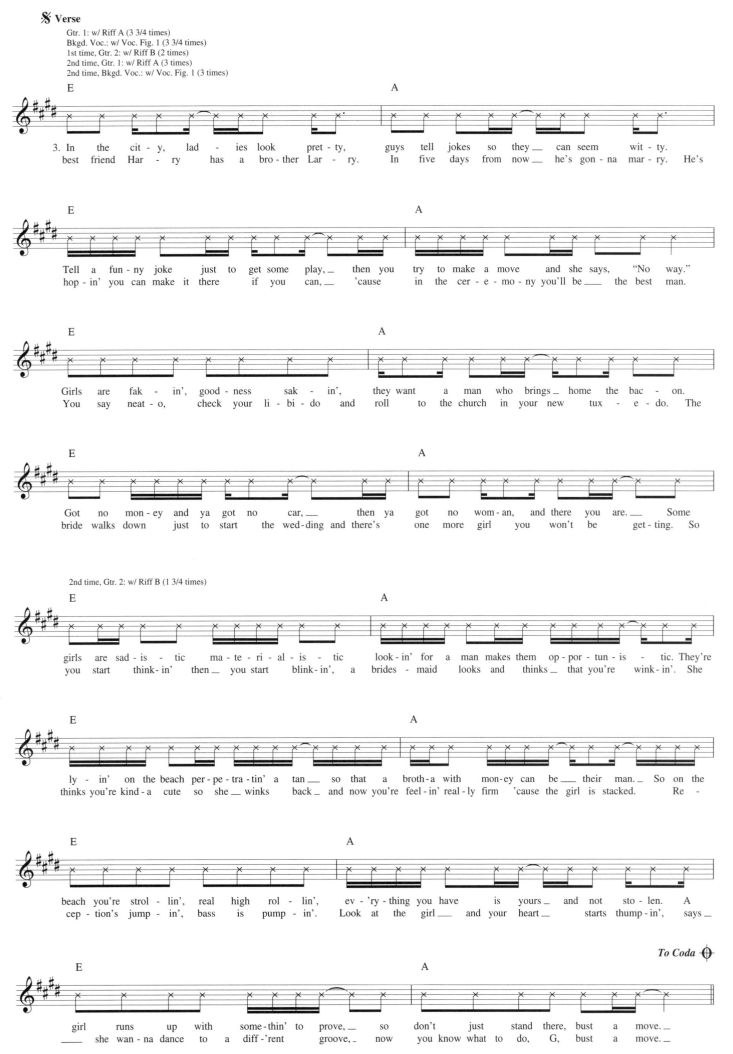

Chorus

Gtr. 1: w/ Riff A (1 3/4 times)
Bkgd. Voc.: w/ Voc. Fig. 1 (1 3/4 times)

If you ___ want it   you got it.   You ___ want it, ba-

(Huh,

Gtr. 2

- by you got it.   You ___ want it,   you got it.

Just bust a move. ___   hey,   ooh,   uh.)

Interlude

Gtr. 2 tacet
w/ Bkgd. Voc. ad lib.

You ___ want it, ba - by you got it.

Break it down for me fel-las.

✛ Coda

Chorus

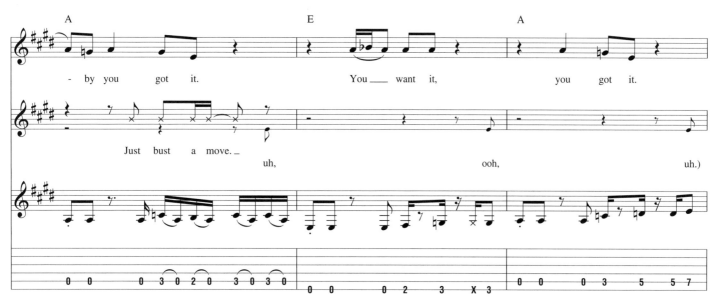

Outro

Gtr. 1: w/ Riff A (1 1/4 times)
Bkgd. Voc.: w/ Voc. Fig. 1 (2 times)

Dancing with Myself

Words and Music by Billy Idol and Tony James

Intro
Fast Rock ♩ = 174

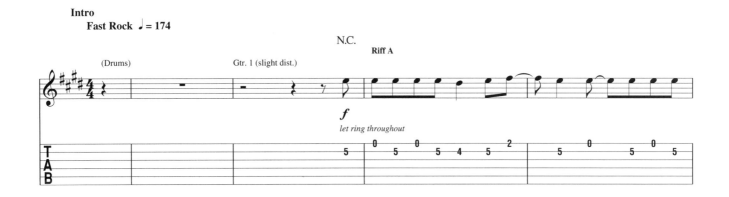

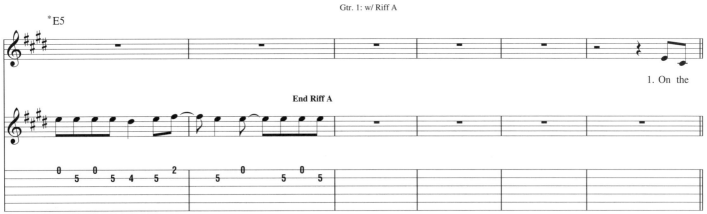

*Chord symbols reflect overall harmony.

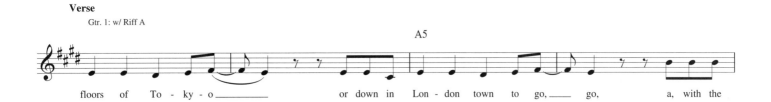

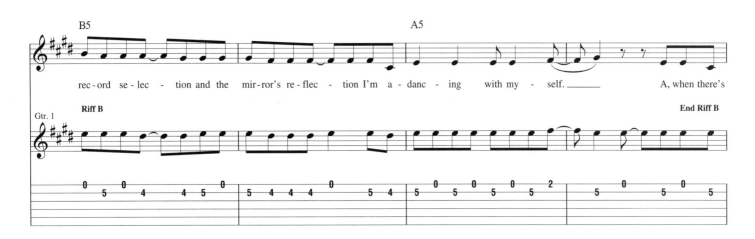

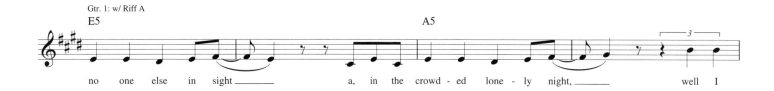

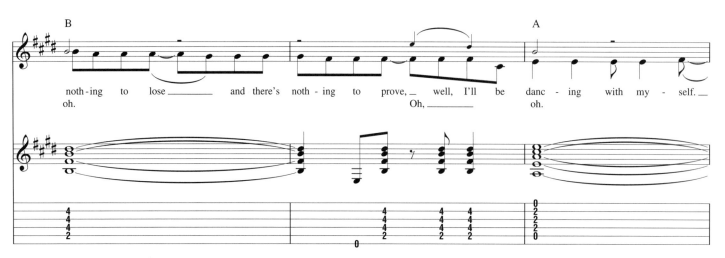

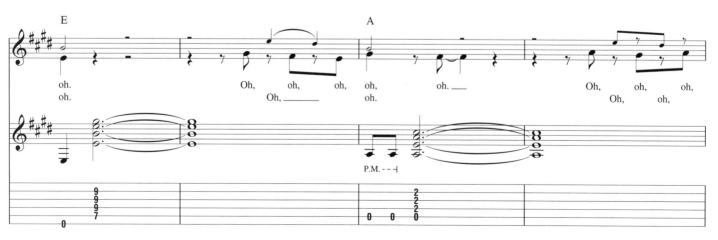

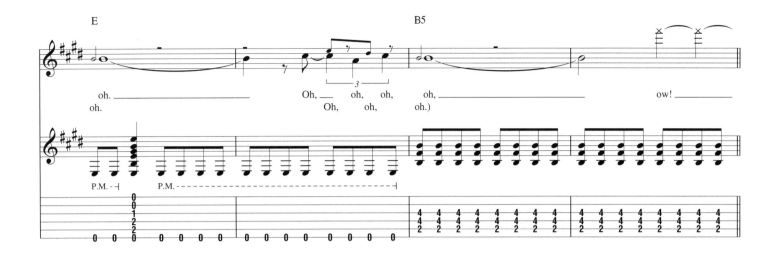

oh. _____ oh. Oh, ___ oh, oh, oh, Oh, oh, oh.) ow!

Guitar Solo

Gtr. 2 tacet

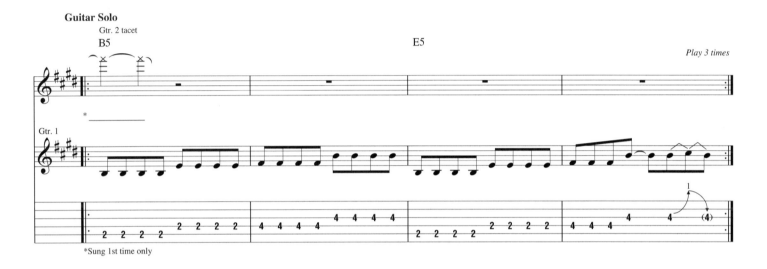

*Sung 1st time only

3. Well, _____ if I

% Verse

Gtr. 1: w/ Riff A
Gtr. 2: w/ Rhy. Fig. 1 (1 1/2 times)

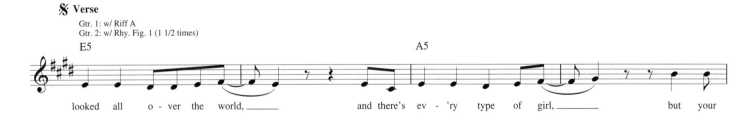

looked all o - ver the world, _____ and there's ev - 'ry type of girl, _____ but your

Gtr. 1: w/ Riff B

emp - ty eyes _____ seem to _____ pass me by, leave me danc - ing with my - self. _____ So let's

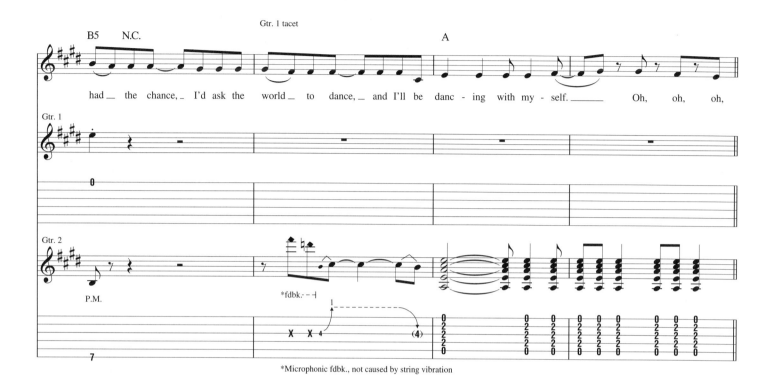

*Microphonic fdbk., not caused by string vibration

Chorus

50

*Voc. Fig. 1

had the chance, I'd ask the world to dance. _____

(Oh, oh, oh,

*Applies to down-stemmed part only.

1st time, Bkgd. Voc.: w/Voc. Fig. 1 (3 times)
2nd time, Bkgd. Voc.: w/ Voc. Fig. 1 (till fade)

E   A

End Voc. Fig. 1

Oh, oh, oh, oh.

Oh, oh, oh,

oh.)

To Coda ⊕

2nd time, Voc.: w/ Voc. Fig. 1

E   A

oh.

Oh, oh, oh, oh.

Oh, oh.

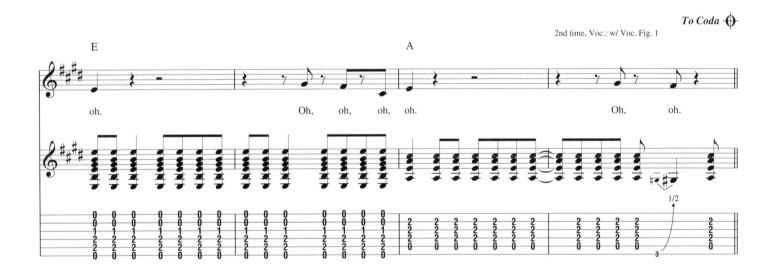

E   A

Voc. Fig. 2   End Voc. Fig. 2

Danc-ing with my-self, _____ oh, oh. Danc-ing with my-self, _____ oh, oh.

Rhy. Fig. 2   End Rhy. Fig. 2

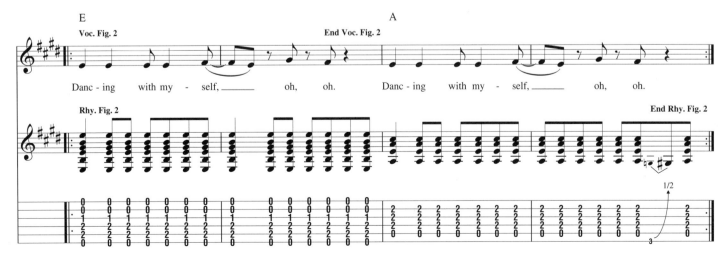

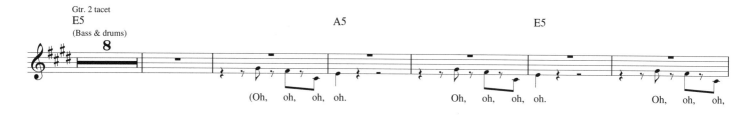

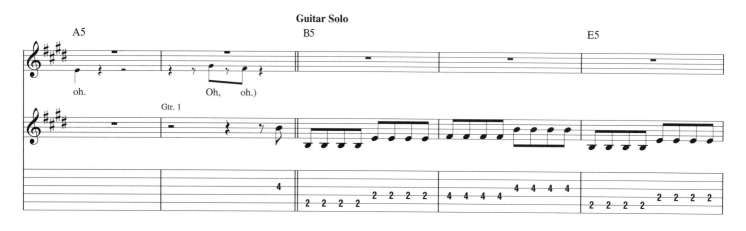

Don't Stop Believin'

Words and Music by Steve Perry, Neal Schon and Jonathan Cain

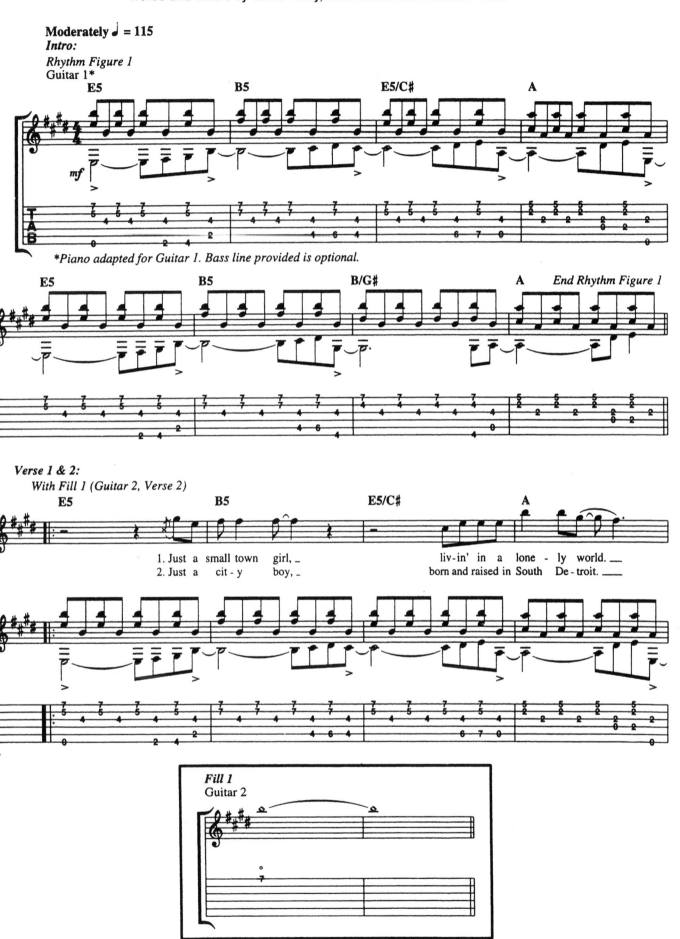

She took the / He took the } mid-night train goin' an - y - where. ____

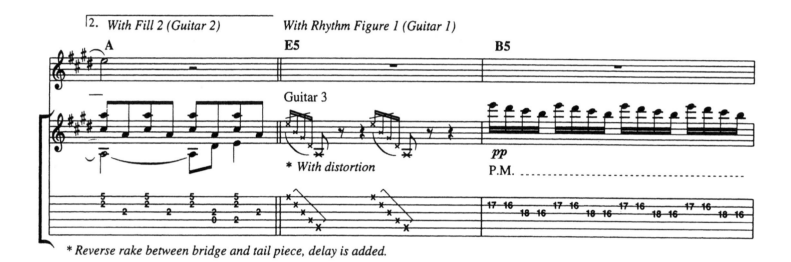

2. With Fill 2 (Guitar 2)   With Rhythm Figure 1 (Guitar 1)

Guitar 3

* With distortion

pp

P.M. -

* Reverse rake between bridge and tail piece, delay is added.

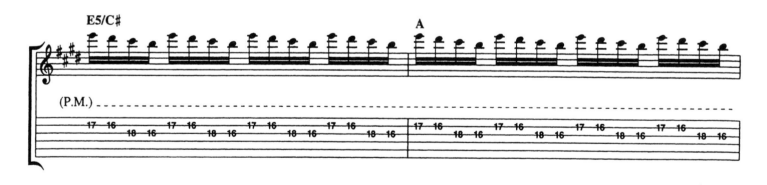

(P.M.) -

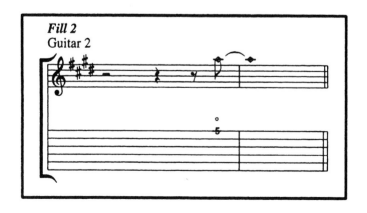

Fill 2
Guitar 2

54

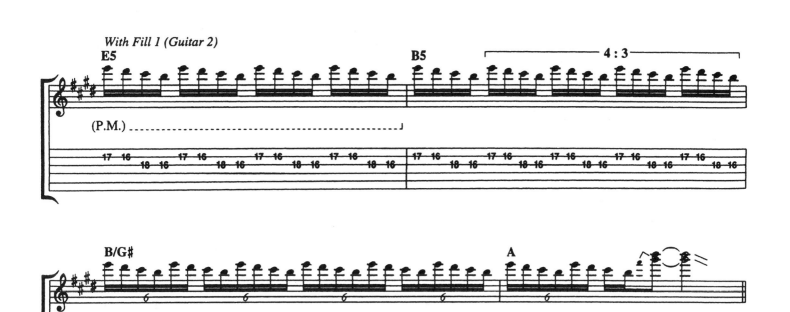

With Fill 1 (Guitar 2)

Verse 3:
With Rhythm Figure 1 (Guitar 1)

3. A sing - er in a smok - y room. _____

The smell of wine and cheap per - fume. _____ For a smile _ they can

share the night; _ It goes on and on _____ and on _____ and on. _____

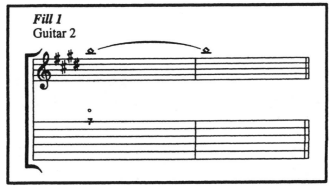

Fill 1
Guitar 2

Verse 5:

With Rhythm Figure 3, w/ ad lib variations (Guitar 5)

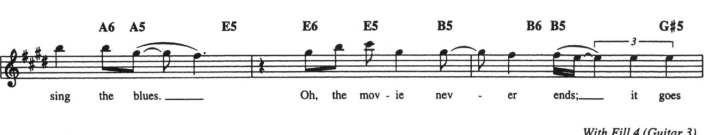

5. Some will win,___ some will lose, ___ some were born to

sing the blues. _____ Oh, the mov - ie nev - er ends;___ it goes

With Fill 4 (Guitar 3)

on and on _____ and on _____ and on. _____

Bridge 2:

With Rhythm Figure 2 (Guitar 4)

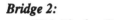

1. Stran - gers ___ wait - ing ___ up and down the boul - e - vard. ___ Their

2. *See additional lyrics*

Guitar 3

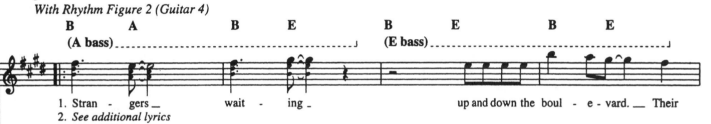

P.M. --

Guitar 5

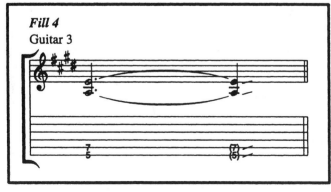

Fill 4
Guitar 3

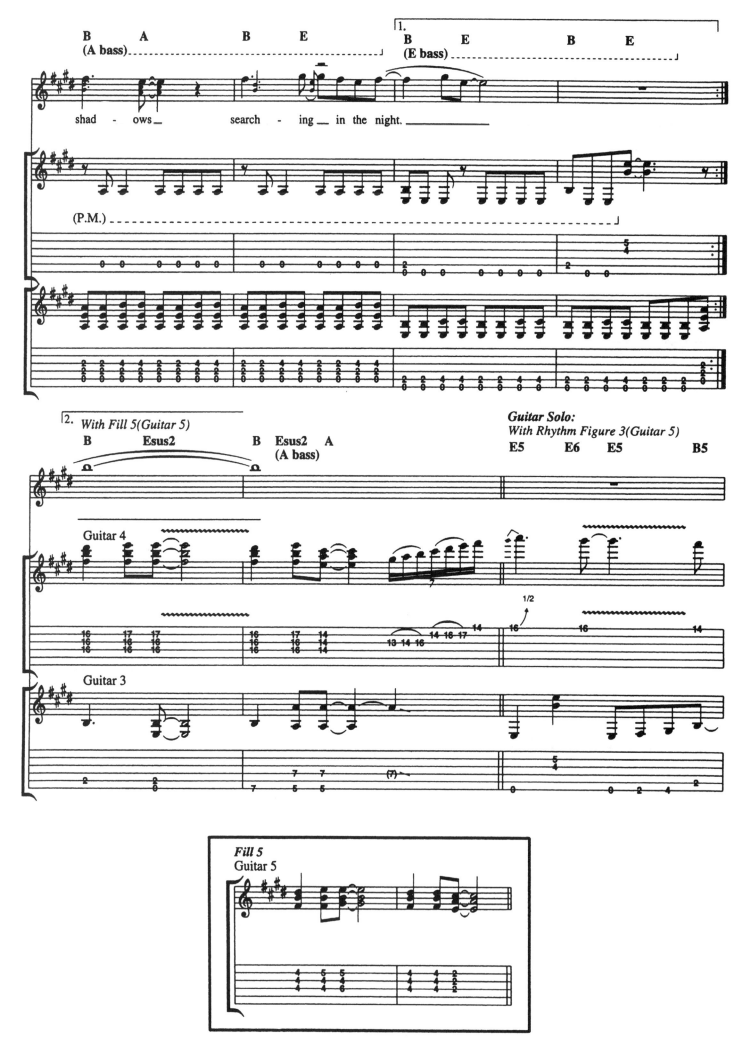

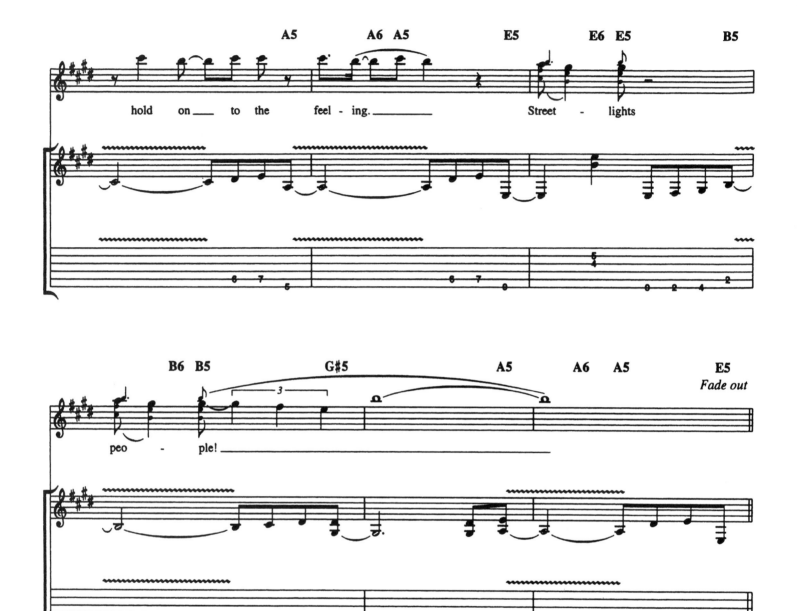

Additional Lyrics

Bridge 1 & 2:

2: Streetlights, people,
    Living just to find emotion.
    Hiding somewhere in the night.

Gives You Hell

Words and Music by Tyson Ritter and Nick Wheeler

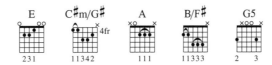

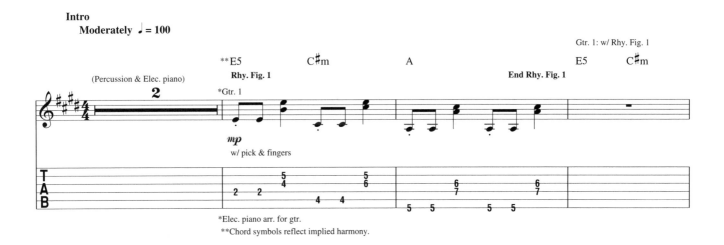

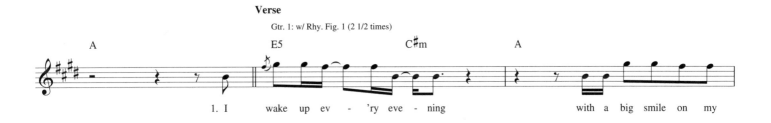

Chorus

face, hope it gives you hell, hope it gives you hell. When you walk my

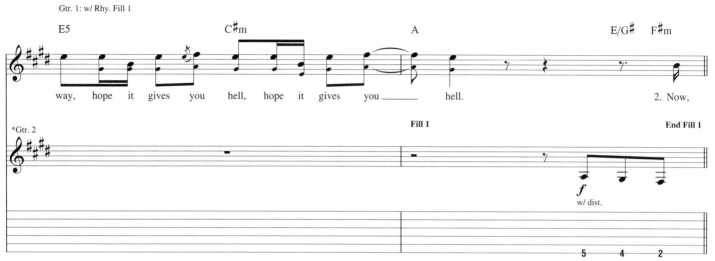

way, hope it gives you hell, hope it gives you _____ hell. 2. Now,

*Gtr. 2

Fill 1   End Fill 1

*Bass arr. for gtr.

Verse

where's your pick - et fence, ____ love? And where's that shin - y car, ___

___ and did it ev - er get you ____ far? You

Rhy. Fig. 2

Gtr. 3 (acous.)

End Rhy. Fig. 2

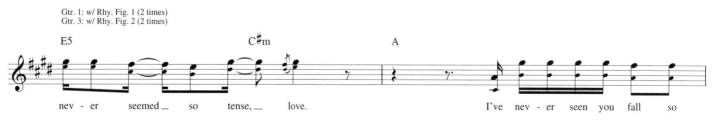

nev - er seemed ___ so tense, ___ love. I've nev - er seen you fall so

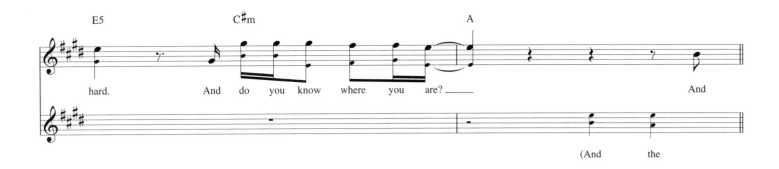

Pre-Chorus

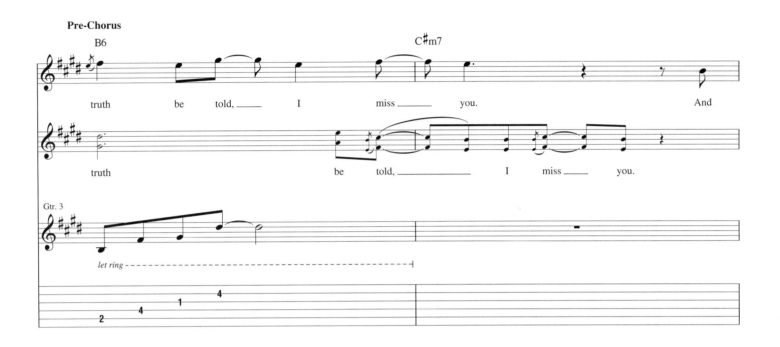

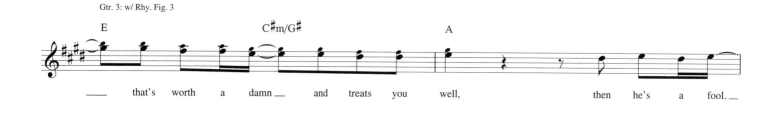

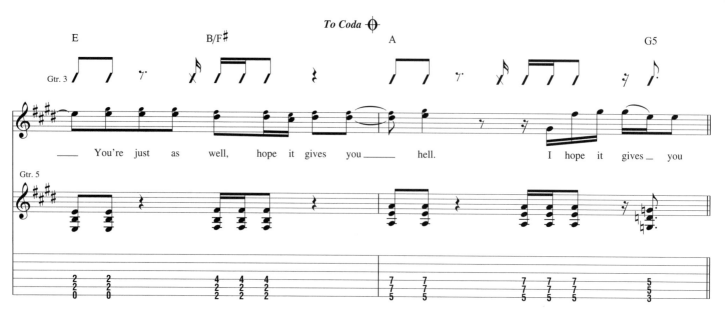

Interlude

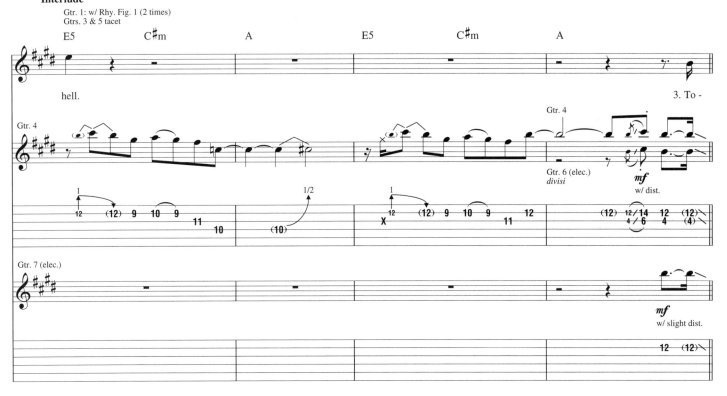

Verse

Pre-Chorus

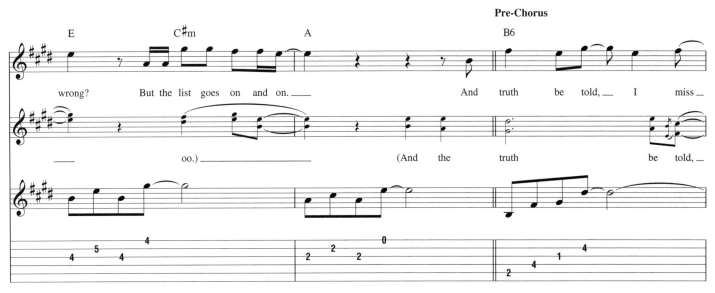

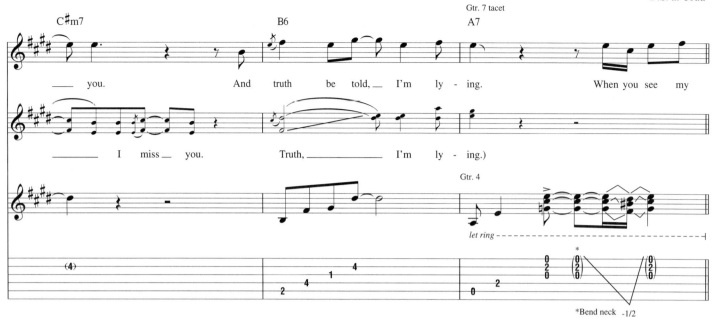

you. And truth be told, I'm ly - ing. When you see my

I miss you. Truth, I'm ly - ing.)

let ring

*Bend neck -1/2

Coda

Bridge

hell. Now, you'll nev-er see what you've done to me. You can

(Oo,

*mf

*Gtr. 2
*Bass arr. for gtr.

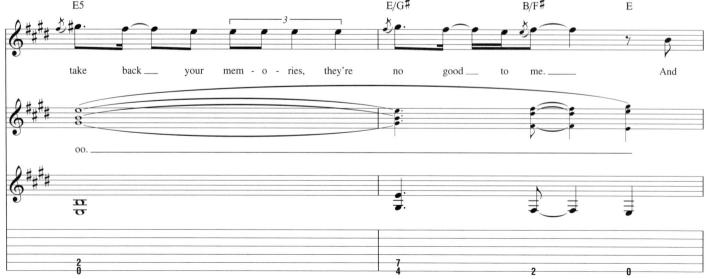

take back your mem - o - ries, they're no good to me. And

oo.

Breakdown

Gtr. 5 tacet

face, hope it gives you hell, hope it gives you hell. When you walk my

Riff A
*Gtr. 2

𝒑

*Bass arr. for gtr.

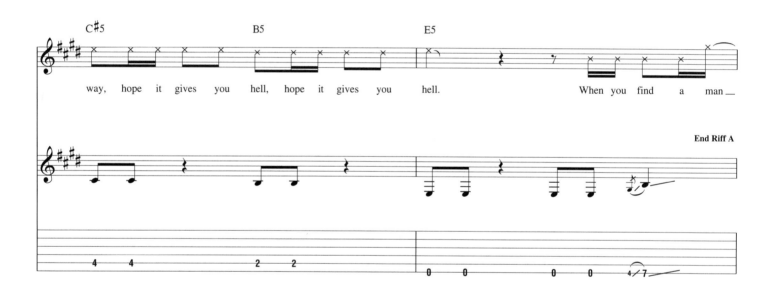

way, hope it gives you hell, hope it gives you hell. When you find a man —

End Riff A

Gtr. 2: w/ Riff A

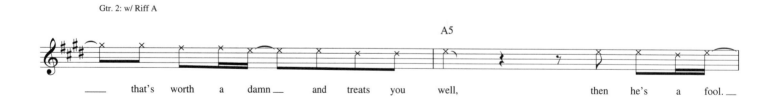

— that's worth a damn — and treats you well, then he's a fool. —

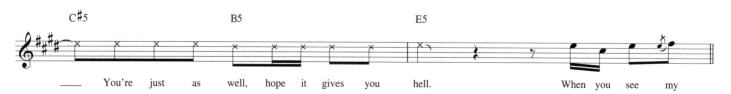

— You're just as well, hope it gives you hell. When you see my

72

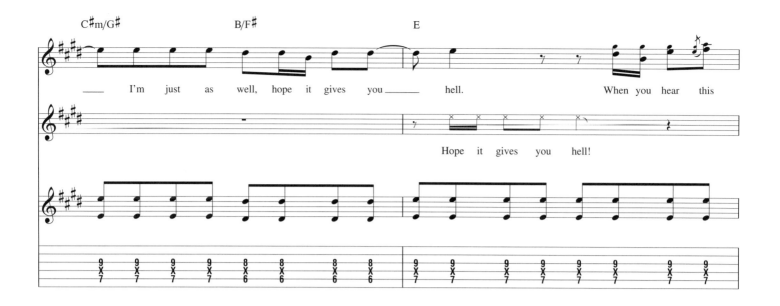

I'm just as well, hope it gives you _____ hell.
Hope it gives you hell!
When you hear this

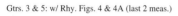

Gtrs. 3 & 5: w/ Rhy. Figs. 4 & 4A (last 2 meas.)

song, I hope that it will give you hell.
Hope it gives you hell!)
You can sing a - long, _____

_____ I hope that it puts you through hell.

Gtr. 10

Gtr. 5

Hello

Words and Music by Lionel Richie

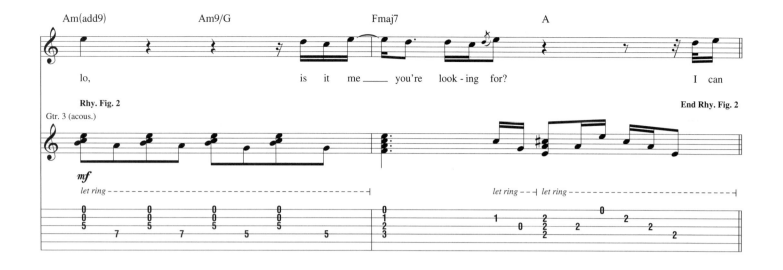

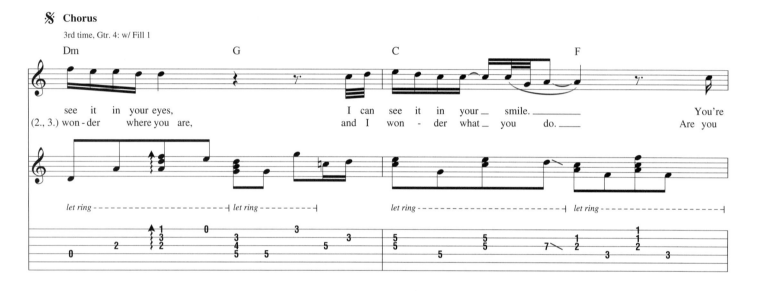

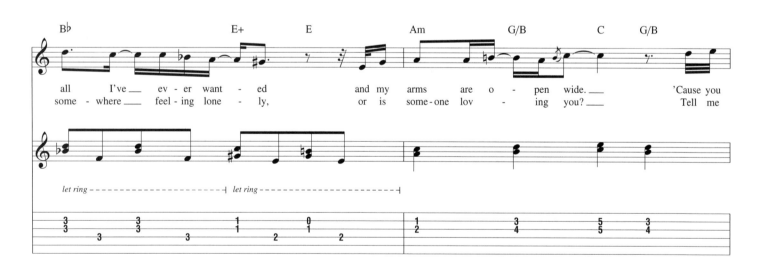

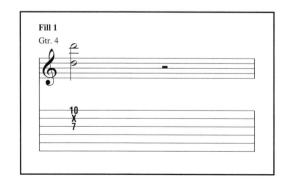

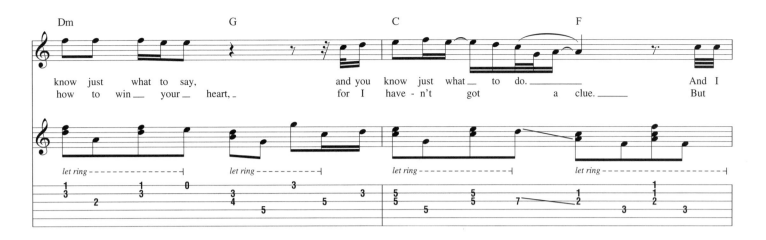

know just what to say,
how to win your heart,
and you know just what to do.
for I have-n't got a clue.
And I
But

To Coda 2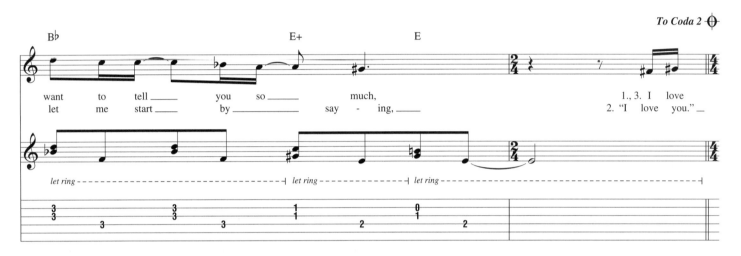

want to tell you so much,
let me start by say - ing,
1., 3. I love
2. "I love you."

Interlude

Gtr. 1: w/ Rhy. Fig. 1

Am(add9)   Am9/G   Fmaj7   Fmaj7/G   Fmaj7

you.

H.H.   H.H.   H.H.

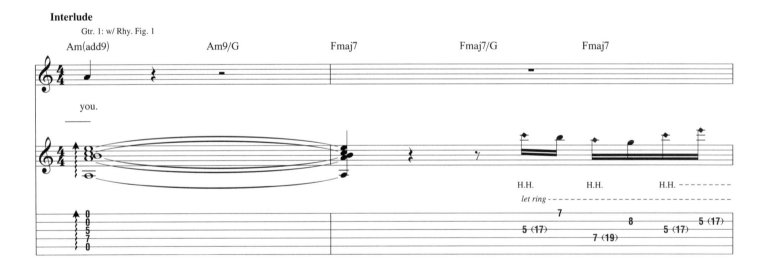

To Coda 1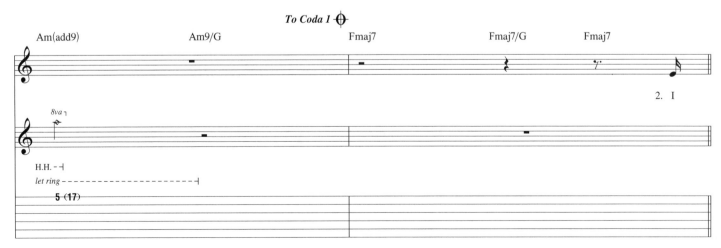

Am(add9)   Am9/G   Fmaj7   Fmaj7/G   Fmaj7

2. I

H.H.

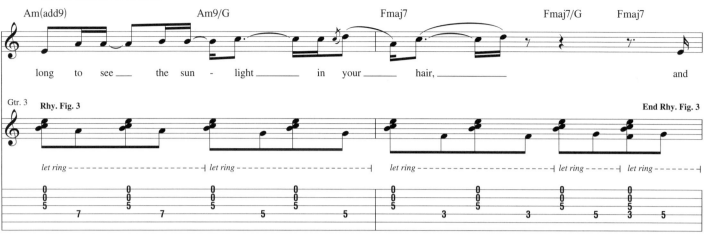

long to see ___ the sun - light _____ in your _____ hair, _____ and

tell you time ___ and time a - gain _____ how much I care. ____ Some -

times I feel ___ my heart ___ will _____ o - ver - flow. _____ Hel -

lo, I've just got to let you know. 'Cause I

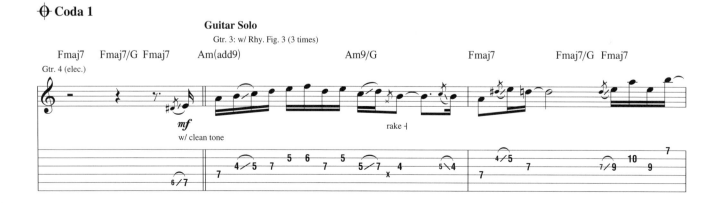

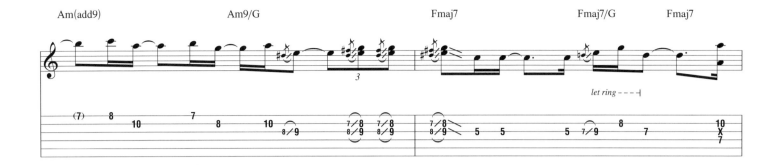

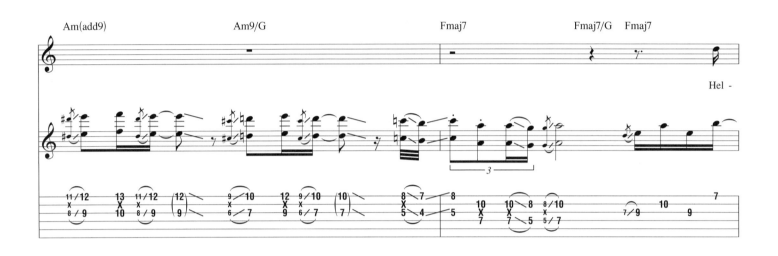

D.S. al Coda 2
(take 2nd lyrics)

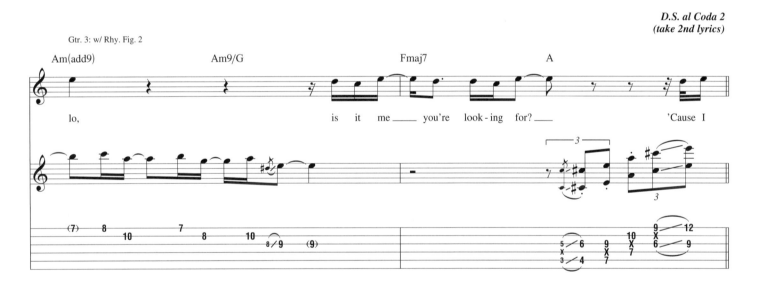

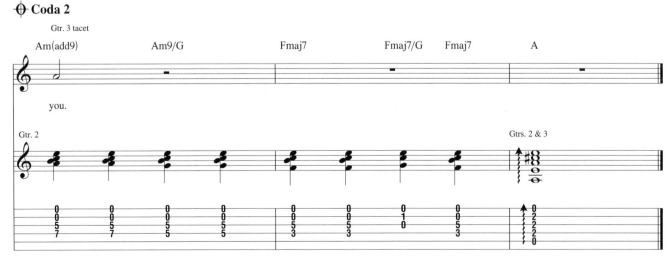

Hello, Goodbye

Words and Music by John Lennon and Paul McCartney

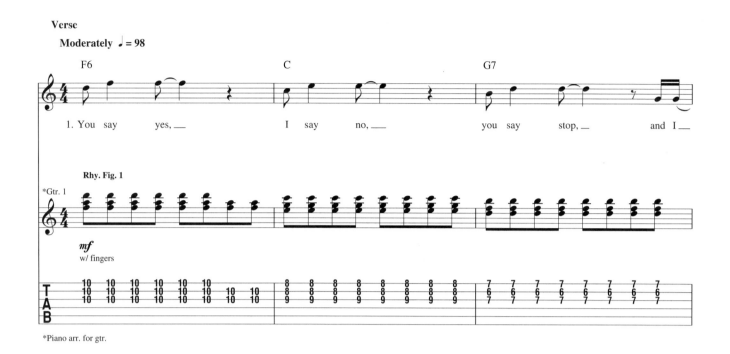

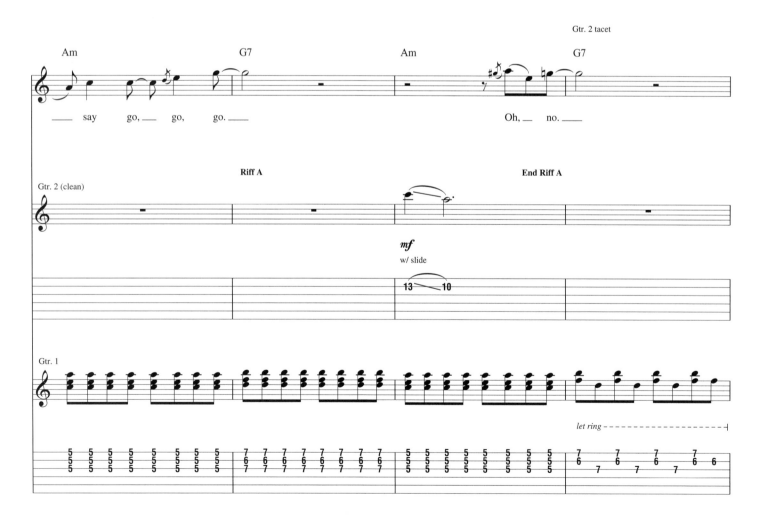

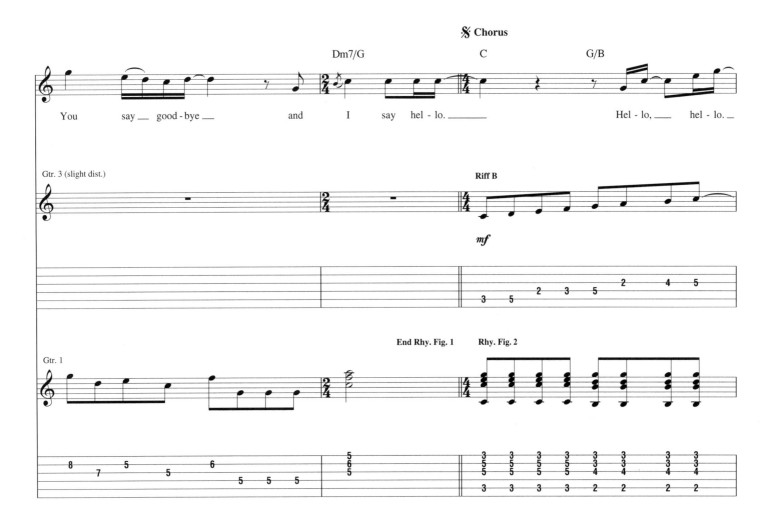

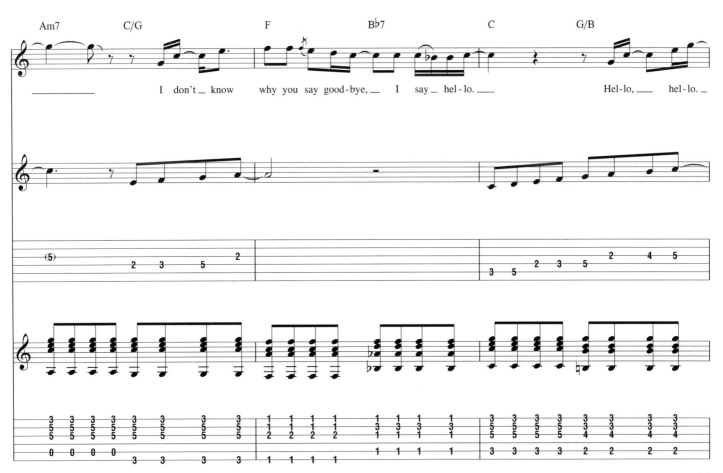

Verse

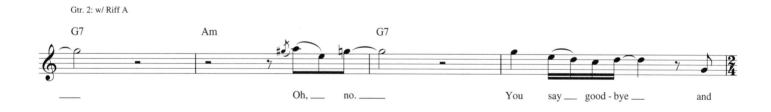

Chorus

why you say good-bye, I say hel-lo. Hel-lo, hel-lo.

Hel-lo, good-bye, hel-lo, good-bye.

I don't know why you say good-bye, I say hel-lo.

Hel-lo, good-bye, hel-lo, good-bye.)

Bridge

Gtr. 1: w. Rhy. Fig. 1

Why, why, why, why, why, why do you say good-bye, good-bye?

*Gtr. 4

mf

*Cello arr. for gtr.

D.S. al Coda

Gtr. 2: w/ Riff A
Gtr. 4 tacet

Bye, bye, bye, bye. Oh, no. You say good-bye and I say hel-lo.

 Coda

Verse

Gtr. 1: w/ Rhy. Fig. 1
Gtr. 3 tacet

3. You say yes, I say no, you say stop, and I

(I say yes, but I may mean no. I can stay

83

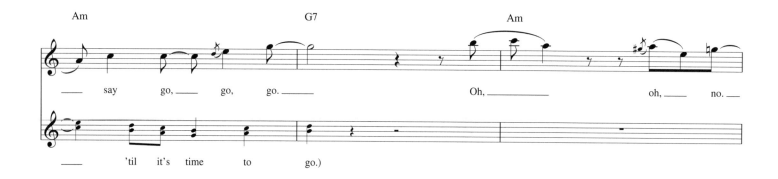

say go, go, go. Oh, oh, no.

('til it's time to go.)

You say good-bye and I say hel-lo.

Chorus

Gtr. 1: w/ Rhy. Fig. 2 (1st 6 meas.)
Gtr. 3: w/ Riff B

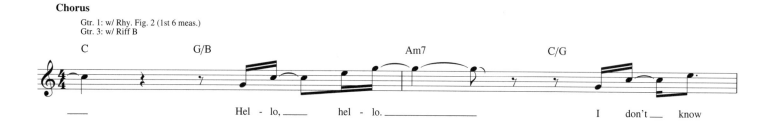

Hel-lo, hel-lo. I don't know

why you say good-bye, I say hel-lo. Hel-lo, hel-lo.

I don't know why you say good-bye, I say hel-lo.

Gtr. 1: w/ Rhy. Fig. 2 (1st 3 meas.)

Hel-lo, hel-lo. I don't know why you say good-bye, I say hel-

Gtr. 3

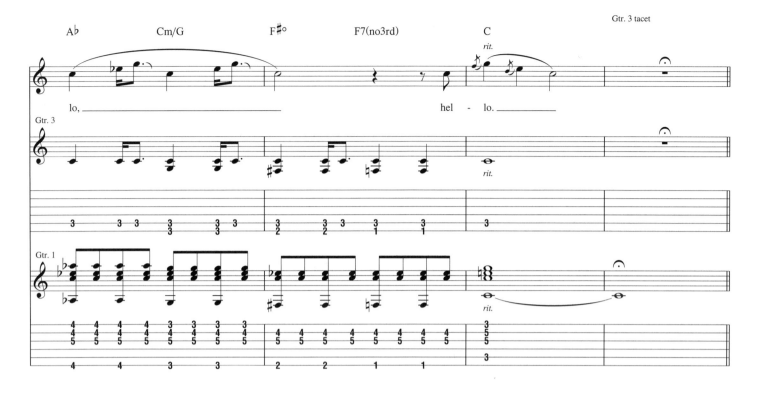

Outro
A tempo

Hey, la, hey, — ba, hel - lo, ah. Hey, la, hey, — ba, hel - lo, ah.

Hey, la, hey, — ba, hel - lo, ah. Hey, la, hey, — ba, hel - lo, ah.

Imagine

Words and Music by John Lennon

Drop D tuning, down 1 step:
(low to high) C-G-C-F-A-D

Intro
Slowly ♩ = 77

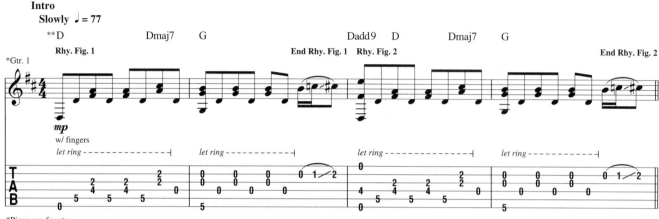

*Gtr. 1

*Piano arr. for gtr.

**Chord symbols reflect implied harmony.

𝄋 Verse

1st & 3rd times, Gtr. 1: w/ Rhy. Fig. 2 (3 1/2 times)
2nd time, Gtr. 1: w/ Rhy. Fig. 1

2nd time, Gtr. 1: w/ Rhy. Fig. 2 (2 1/2 times)

***Sing cue, 2nd time.

1. Im-ag-ine there's no heav-en, it's eas-y if you try.
2. Im-ag-ine there is no coun-tries, it is-n't hard to do.
3. Im-ag-ine no pos-ses-sions, I won-der if you can.

No hell be-low us, a-bove us on-ly sky.
Noth-ing to kill or die for, and no re-li-gion too.
No need for greed or hun-ger, a broth-er-hood of man.

Pre-Chorus

Im-ag-ine all the peo-ple

liv-in' for to-day.
liv-in' life in peace.
shar-ing all the world.

Gtr. 1

Jump

Words and Music by David Lee Roth, Edward Van Halen, Alex Van Halen and Michael Anthony

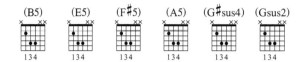

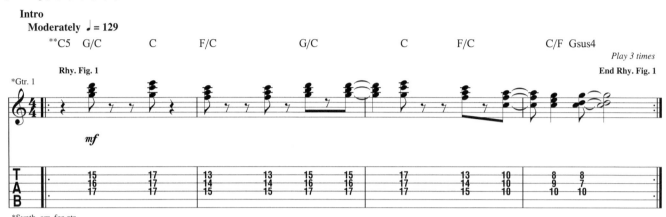

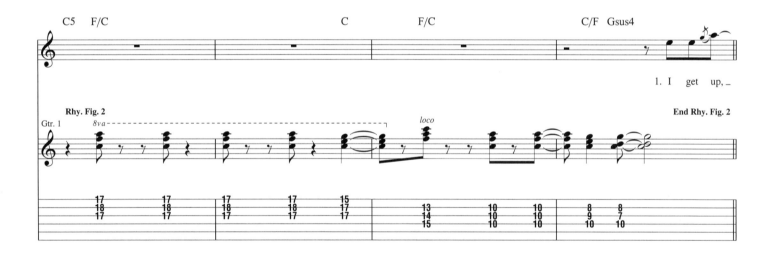

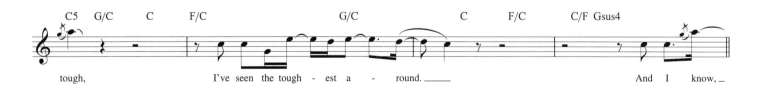

Gtr. 1: w/ Rhy. Fig. 1 (2 times)

C5 G/C C F/C G/C C F/C C/F Gsus4

___ ___ "Hey you!" __ "Who said that?" __ ba-by, just __ how you feel. __ You got to
___ ___ Ba-by how __ you been? You say you don't

C5 G/C C F/C G/C C F/C C/F Gsus4

roll _____ with the punch-es and get to what's real. __ Ah, can't ya
know, _____ you won't __ know _____ un-til you be-gin. __ So can't ya

Pre-Chorus

Am F C Dm
*(G#m) (E) (B) (C#m)

see me stand-in' here, I got my back a-gainst the rec-ord ma-chine. _____

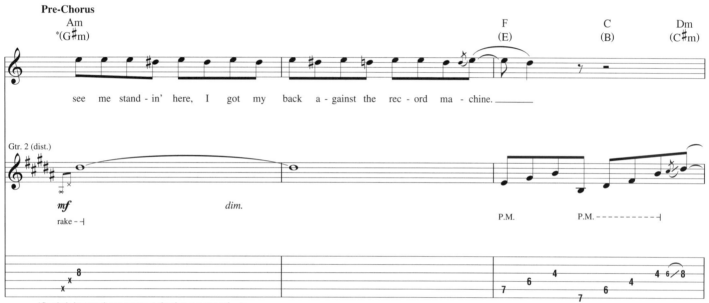

Gtr. 2 (dist.)

mf *dim.*

rake

P.M. P.M. - - - - - - - - - -

*Symbols in parentheses represent chord names respective to altered tuned guitars. Symbols above reflect actual sounding chords.

F C Dm
(E) (B) (C#m)

I ain't the worst that you've seen. _____ Ah, can't ya see what I mean? __

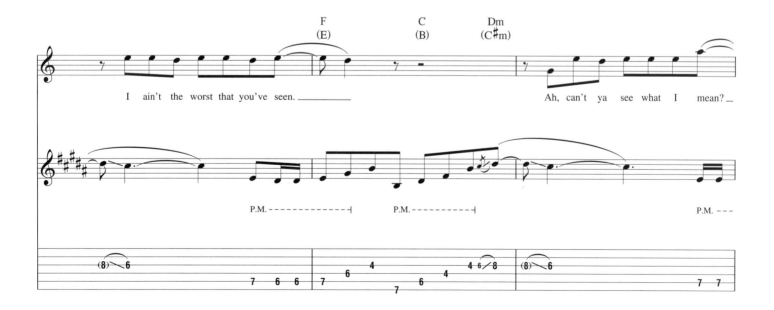

P.M. - - - - - - - - - -| P.M. - - - - - - - - - -| P.M. - - -

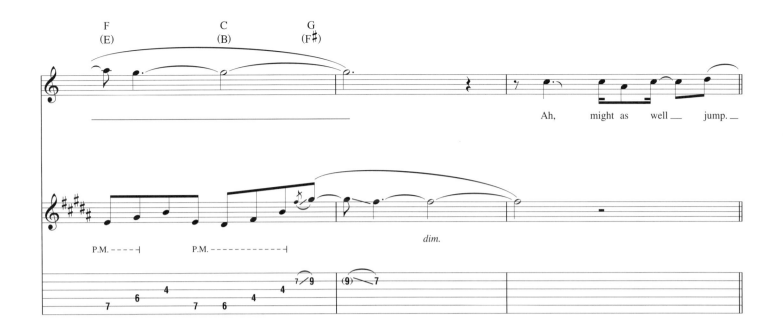

Ah, might as well ___ jump. ___

Chorus

Gtr. 1: w/ Rhy. Fig. 1
Gtr. 2 tacet

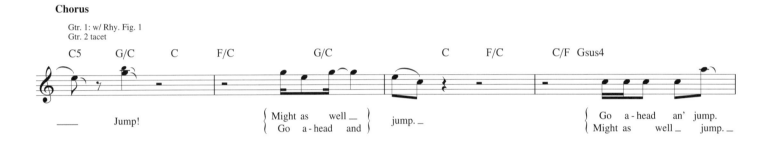

___ Jump!

{ Might as well ___ }
{ Go a-head and } jump. ___

{ Go a-head an' jump.
{ Might as well ___ jump. ___

2nd time, Gtr. 1: w/ Rhy. Fig. 1

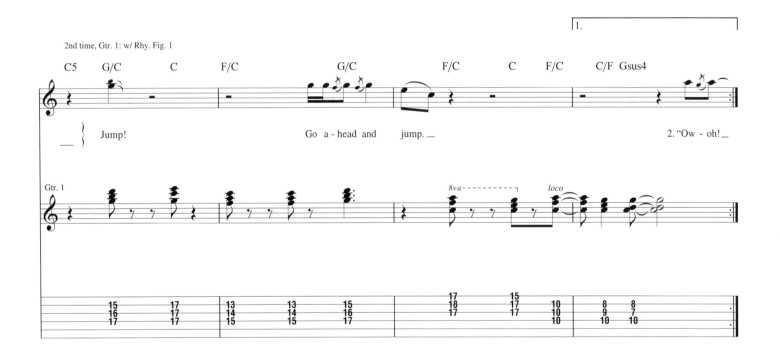

___ Jump!   Go a-head and jump. ___   2. "Ow - oh! ___

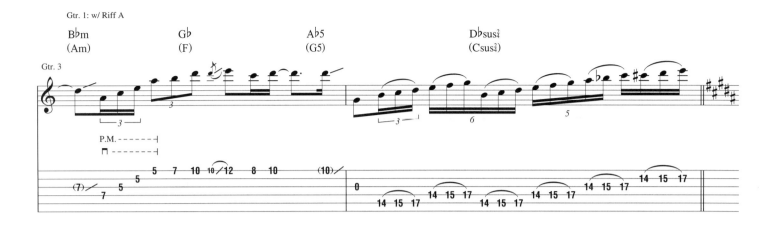

Synth. Solo

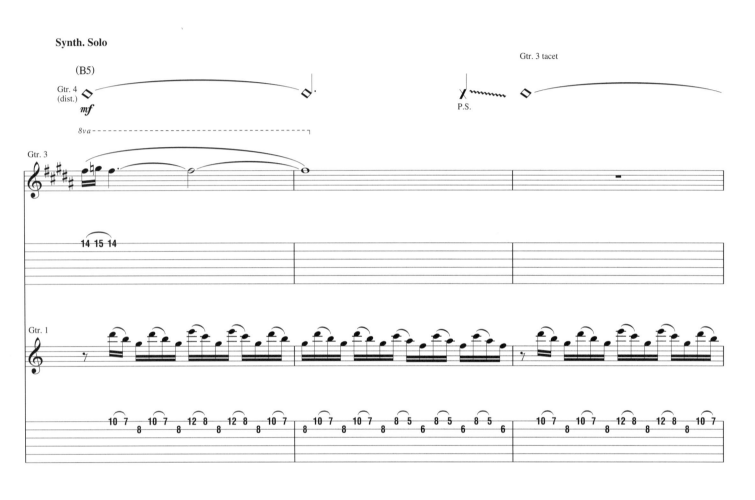

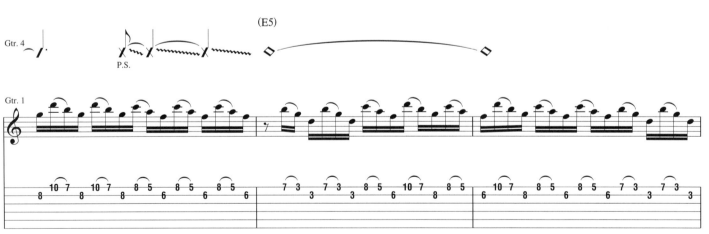

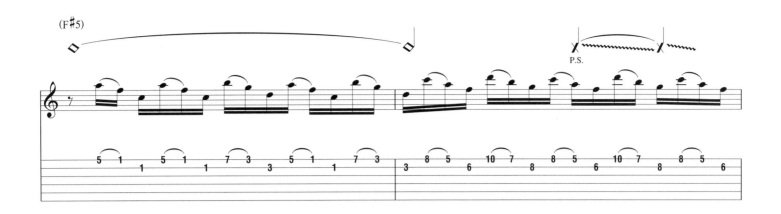

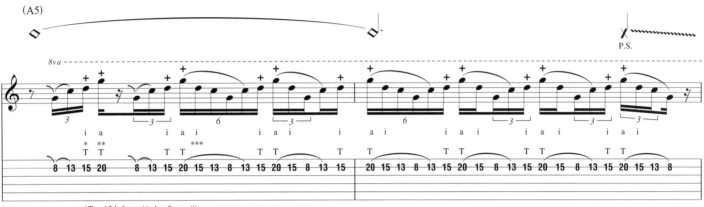

*Tap 15th fret w/ index finger (i).

**Tap 20th fret with ring finger (a).

***Pull off ring finger to index finger.

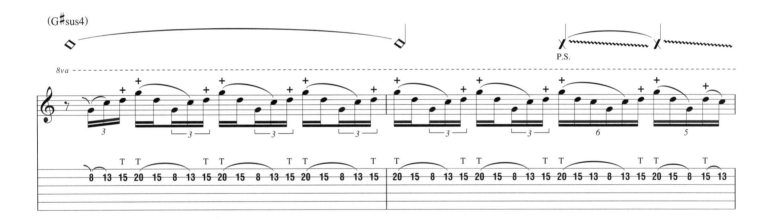

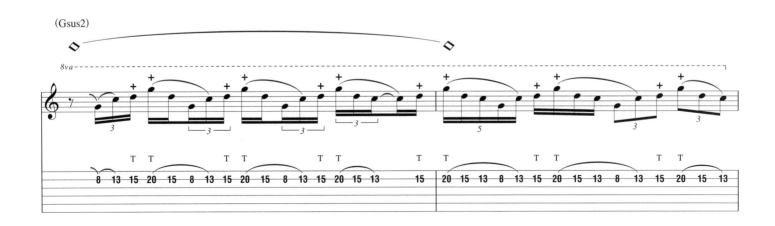

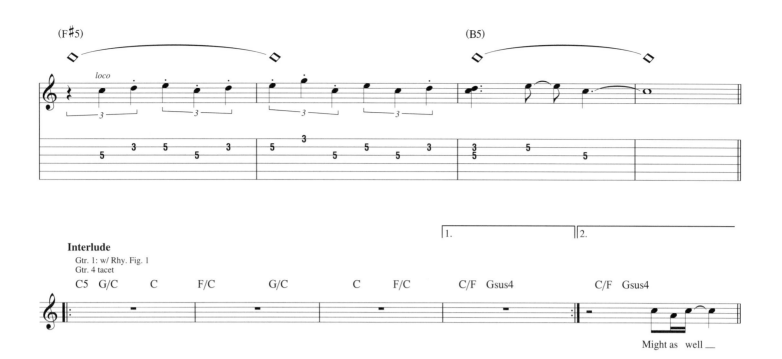

Interlude

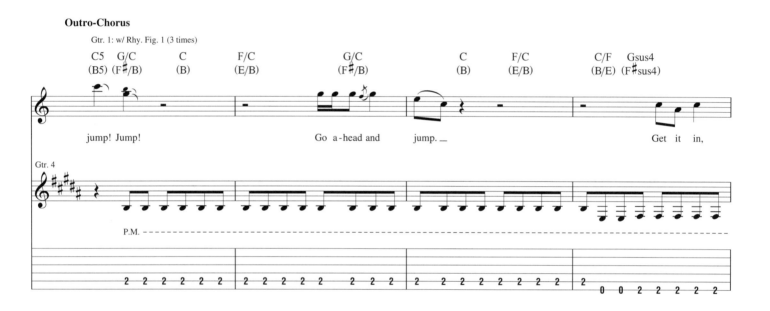

Outro-Chorus

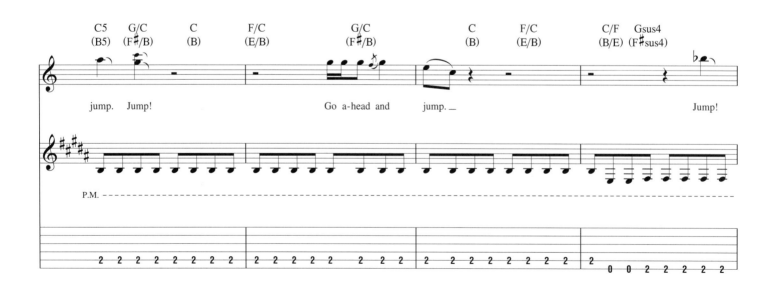

Loser

Words by Beck Hansen
Music by Beck Hansen and Karl Stephenson

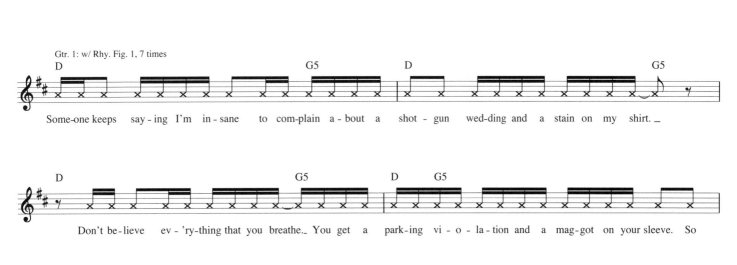

Gtr. 1: w/ Rhy. Fig. 1, 7 times

Some-one keeps say-ing I'm in-sane to com-plain a-bout a shot-gun wed-ding and a stain on my shirt. _

Don't be-lieve ev-'ry-thing that you breathe._ You get a park-ing vi-o-la-tion and a mag-got on your sleeve. So

Gtr. 2 tacet

shave your face _ with some mace in the dark. _ Sav-ing all your food stamps and burn-ing down the trail-er park.

Chorus

Gtr. 1: w/ Rhy. Fill 2

Gtr. 1: w/ Rhy. Fig. 1, 8 times
Gtr. 2: w/ Riff A, 4 times

Yo. Cut it. Soy _ un per-di-dor._ I'm a

*w/ multi-tracked vocals on Chorus and Bridge sections

los-er, ba - by, ___ so why _ don't you kill me?_ Soy ___ un

Spoken: Double barrel buck shy.

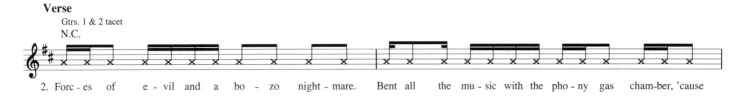

per-di-dor. _ I'm a los-er, ba - by, ___ so why _ don't you kill me? _

Verse

Gtrs. 1 & 2 tacet

N.C.

2. Forc-es of e - vil and a bo-zo night-mare. Bent all the mu-sic with the pho-ny gas cham-ber, 'cause

ones' got a wea-sel and an-oth-er's got a flag. One's on the pole; shove the oth-er in a bag with the

Rhy. Fill 2

Gtr. 1

Proud Mary

Words and Music by John Fogerty

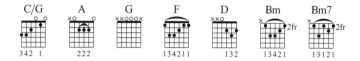

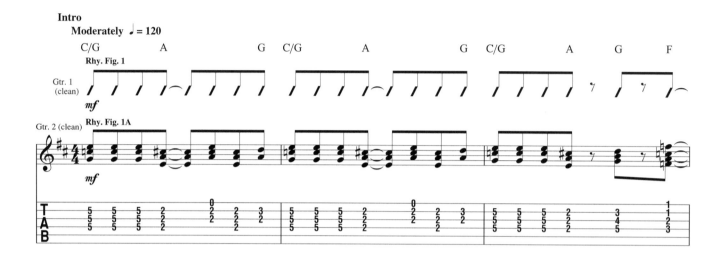

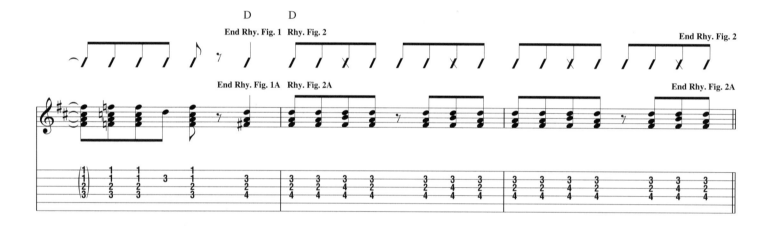

Verse

Gtrs. 1 & 2: w/ Rhy. Figs. 2 & 2A (4 times)

1. Left a good job __ in the cit __ y,   work - in' for the man __ ev - 'ry night and day __
2. Cleaned a lot of __ plates in Mem - phis,   pumped a lot of pain __ down in New Or - leans __
3. If you come down __ to the riv - er,   bet you're gon - na find __ some peo - ple who live.

and I nev - er lost __ one min - ute of sleep - in',   wor - ry - in' 'bout the way __ things might have been. __
but I nev - er saw __ the good __ side of the cit - y   till I hitched a ride __ on a riv - er boat queen.
You don't have to wor - ry 'cause __ you have no mon - ey,   peo - ple on a riv - er are hap - py to give. __

Pre-Chorus

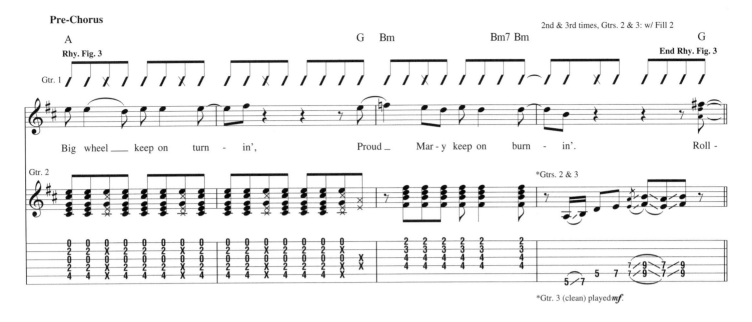

Big wheel ___ keep on turn - in', Proud ___ Mar - y keep on burn - in'. Roll -

*Gtr. 3 (clean) played *mf*.

Chorus

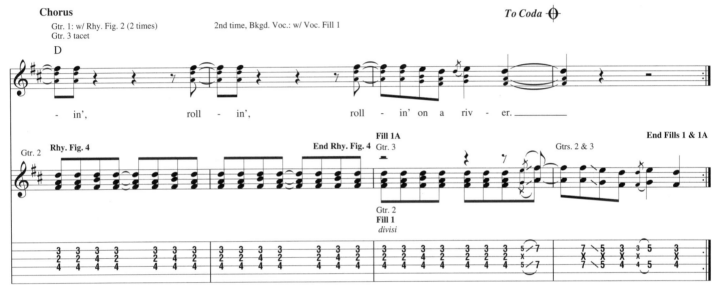

- in', roll - in', roll - in' on a riv - er. ___

(Oh ___ Lord!)

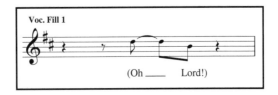

Gtrs. 1 & 2: w/ Rhy. Figs. 1 & 1A
Gtr. 3 tacet

Gtrs. 1 & 2: w/ Rhy. Figs. 2 & 2A

Guitar Solo

Gtr. 1: w/ Rhy. Fig. 2 (4 times)

*Gtrs. 2 & 3

*Composite arrangement

Gtr. 1: w/ Rhy. Fig. 3

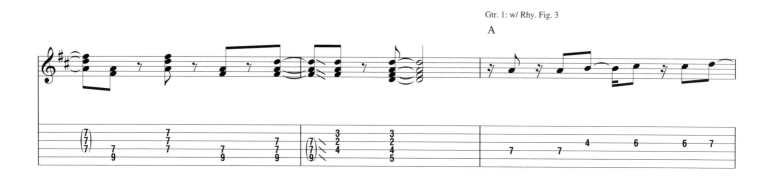

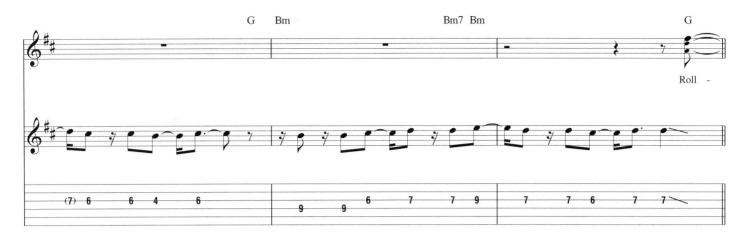

Chorus

Gtr. 1: w/ Rhy. Fig. 2
Gtr. 2: w/ Rhy. Fig. 4
Gtr. 3 tacet

Gtrs. 2 & 3: w/ Fills 1 & 1A

D.C. al Coda

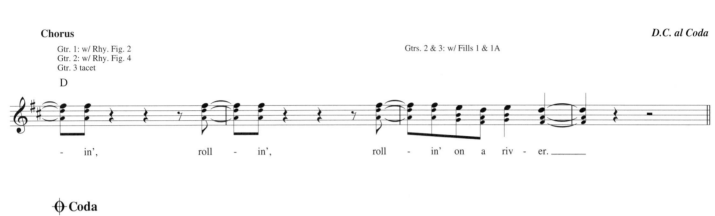

- in', roll - in', roll - in' on a riv - er. _____

Coda

Gtrs. 2 & 3: w/ Fills 1 & 1A (2nd meas.)

Bkgd. Voc.: w/ Voc. Fill 1
Gtr. 1: w/ Rhy. Fig. 2 (till fade)
Gtr. 2: w/ Rhy. Fig. 4

_____ Roll - in', roll - in', roll -

Gtrs. 2 & 3: w/ Fills 1 & 1A

Gtr. 2: w/ Rhy. Fig. 4

- in' on a riv - er. _____ Roll - in', roll -
(Mmm, _____

Begin fade

Gtrs. 2 & 3: w/ Fills 1 & 1A

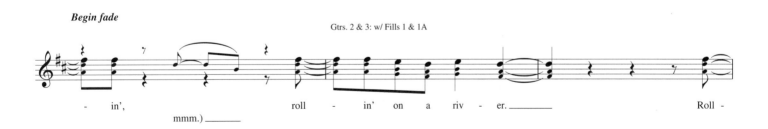

- in', roll - in' on a riv - er. _____ Roll -
mmm.) _____

Fade out

Gtr. 2: w/ Rhy. Fig. 4

Gtrs. 2 & 3: w/ Fills 1 & 1A

- in', roll - in', roll - in' on a riv - er. _____

Somebody to Love

Words and Music by Freddie Mercury

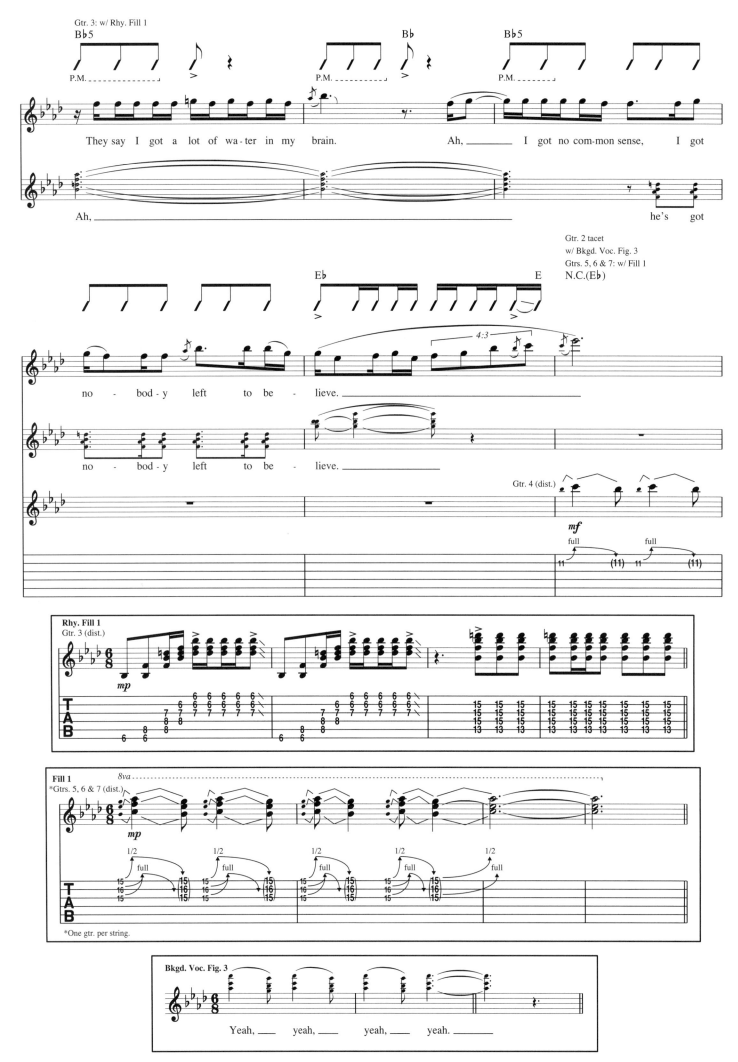

Guitar Solo

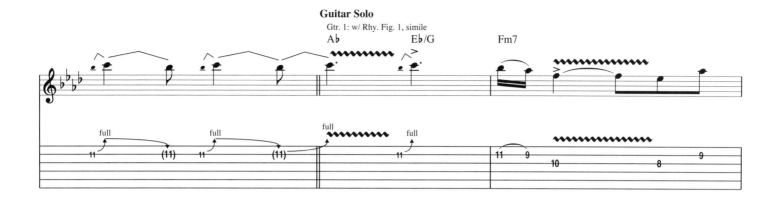

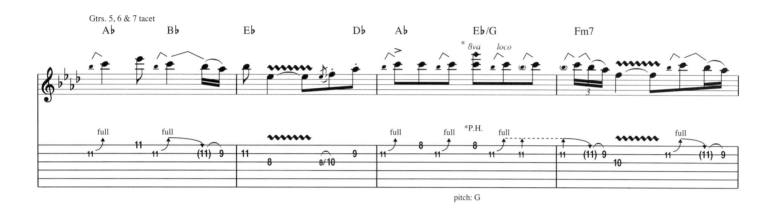

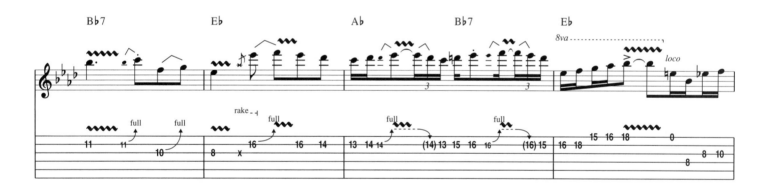

Chorus

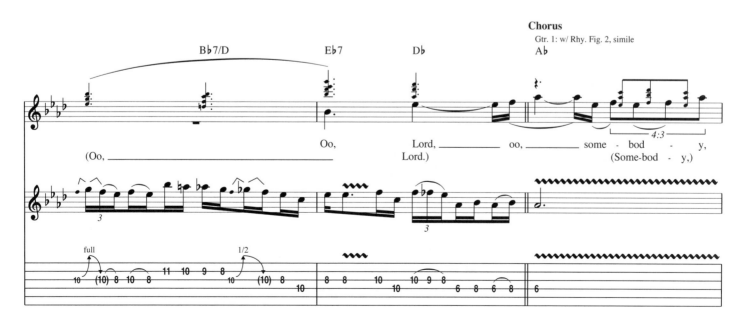

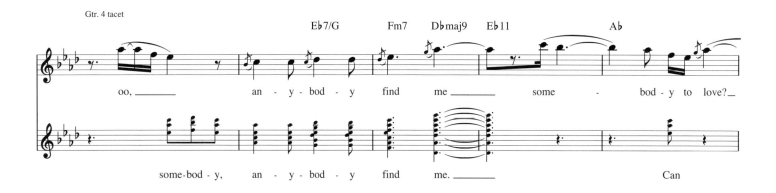

Gtr. 4 tacet

Eb7/G · Fm7 · Dbmaj9 · Eb11 · Ab

oo, _____ an - y - bod - y find me _____ some - bod - y to love?_____

some-bod - y, an - y - bod - y find me. _____ Can

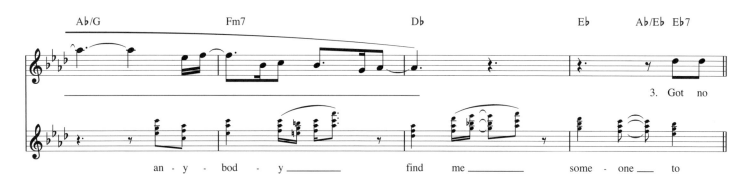

Ab/G · Fm7 · Db · Eb · Ab/Eb · Eb7

3. Got no

an - y - bod - y _____ find me _____ some - one _____ to

Verse

Gtr. 1: w/ Rhy. Fig. 1, simile

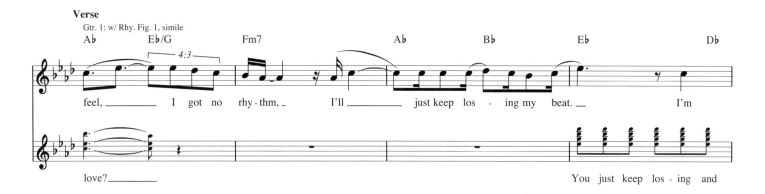

Ab · Eb/G · Fm7 · Ab · Bb · Eb · Db

feel, _____ I got no rhy - thm, _ I'll just keep los - ing my beat. _ I'm

love?_____

You just keep los - ing and

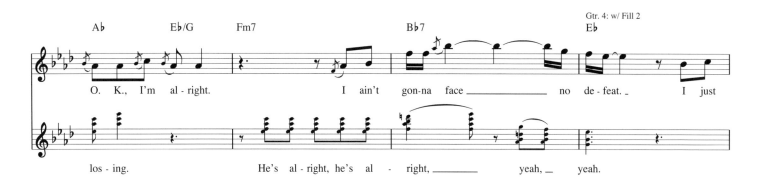

Gtr. 4: w/ Fill 2

Ab · Eb/G · Fm7 · Bb7 · Eb

O. K., I'm al - right. I ain't gon-na face _____ no de - feat. _ I just

los - ing. He's al - right, he's al - right, _____ yeah, _ yeah.

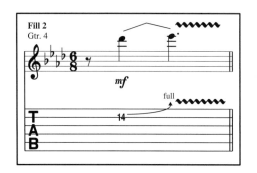

Fill 2
Gtr. 4

mf

full

14

110

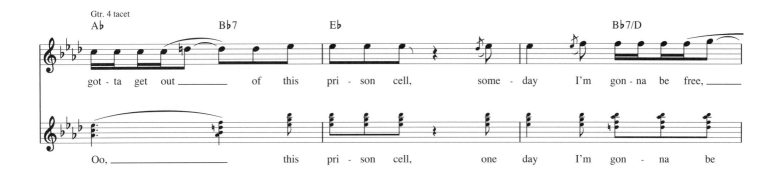

got - ta get out _____ of this pri - son cell, some - day I'm gon - na be free, _____

Oo, _____ this pri - son cell, one day I'm gon - na be

Chorus

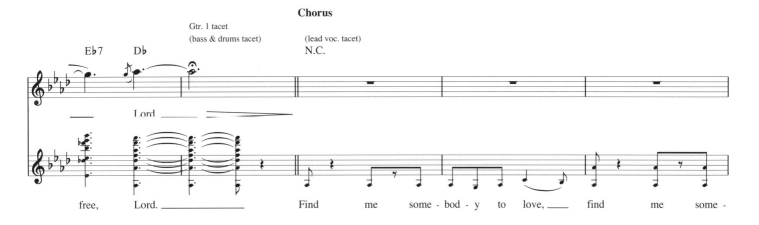

free, Lord. _____ Find me some - bod - y to love, _____ find me some -

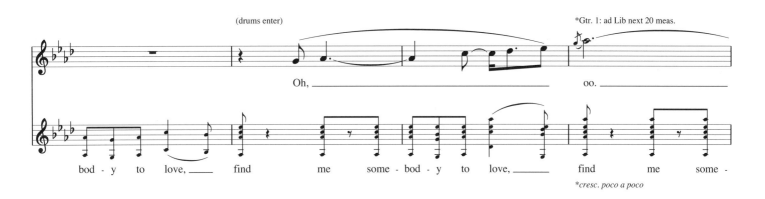

Oh, _____ oo. _____

bod - y to love, _____ find me some - bod - y to love, _____ find me some -

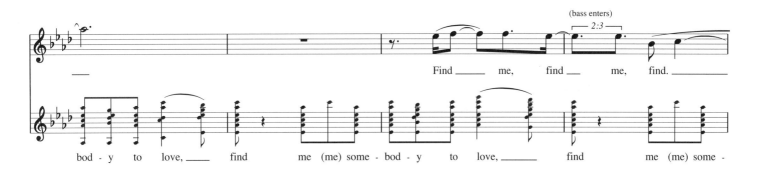

Find _____ me, find _____ me, find. _____

bod - y to love, _____ find me (me) some - bod - y to love, _____ find me (me) some -

Oo, _____ find

bod - y to love, _____ find me (me) some - bod - y to love, _____ find me (me) some - bod - y to love, _____

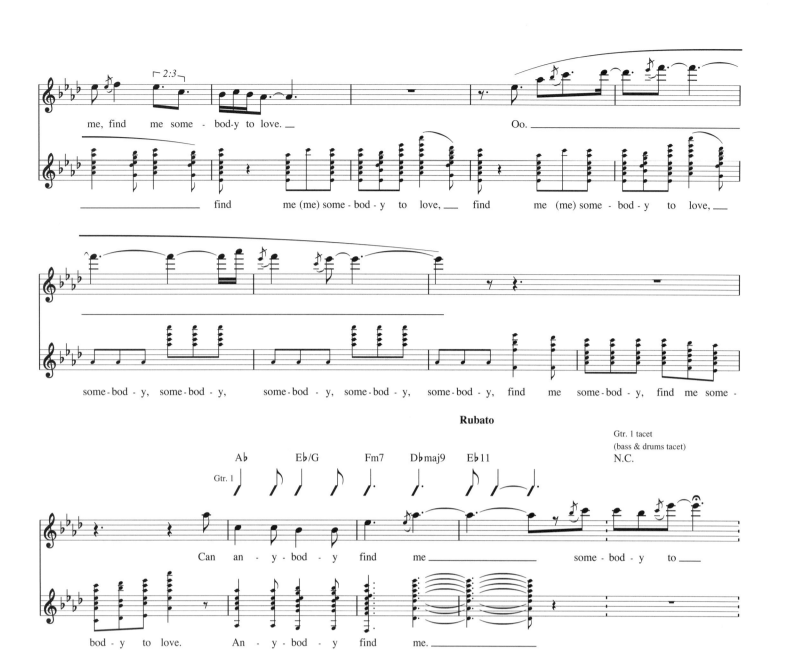

Rubato

Gtr. 1 tacet
(bass & drums tacet)
N.C.

Outro-Chorus
A Tempo
Gtr. 1: w/ Rhy. Fig. 3, 7 times, simile

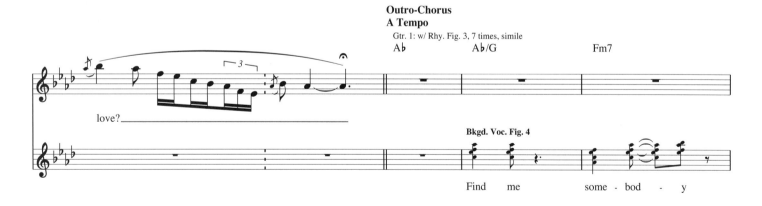

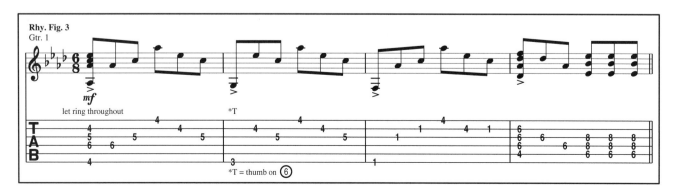

You Keep Me Hangin' On

Words and Music by Edward Holland, Lamont Dozier and Brian Holland

⊕ Coda

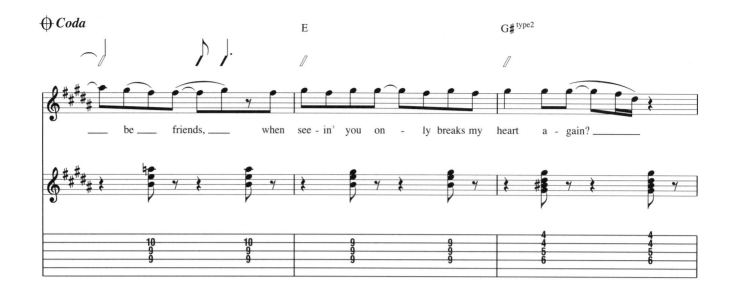

be __ friends, __ when see-in' you on-ly breaks my heart a-gain? __

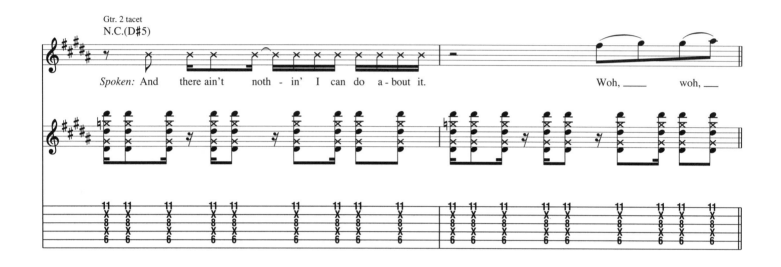

Spoken: And there ain't noth-in' I can do a-bout it. Woh, __ woh, __

Chorus

woh. _____ (Set me free, __ why don't __ ya babe?) Woh, __ woh, __ woh. _____ why don't Get out of my life, __ ...)

__ ya, ba — by? Set me free, why don't __ ya, ba — by?

Verse

Get out of my life, why don't __ ya, ba — by? 3. You claim __ you still __

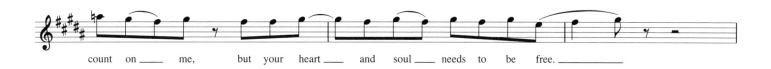

count on ___ me, but your heart ___ and soul ___ needs to be free. ___

And now that you've ___ got ___ your free - dom, you wan - na still hold on to me. ___

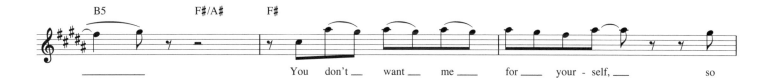

___ You don't ___ want ___ me ___ for ___ your - self, ___ so

Chorus

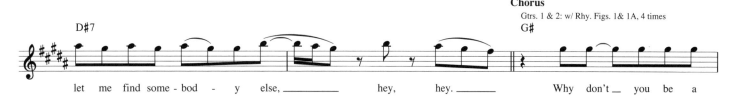

let me find some - bod - y else, ___ hey, hey. ___ Why don't ___ you be a

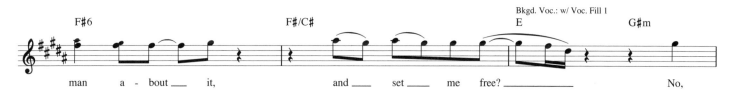

man a - bout ___ it, and ___ set ___ me free? ___ No,

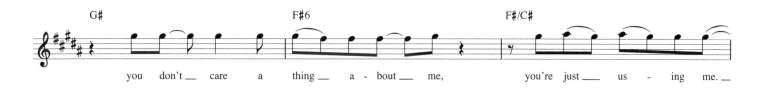

you don't ___ care a thing ___ a - bout ___ me, you're just ___ us - ing me. ___

___ Go on, get up, get out ___ of my life, ___

Begin Fade

and let me sleep at night. ___ 'Cause you don't ___ real - ly love ___

Fade Out

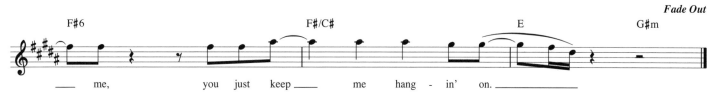

___ me, you just keep ___ me hang - in' on. ___

117

GUITAR NOTATION LEGEND

Guitar music can be notated three different ways: on a *musical staff*, in *tablature*, and in *rhythm slashes*.

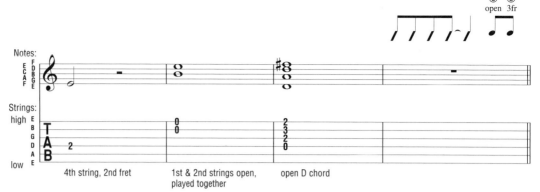

RHYTHM SLASHES are written above the staff. Strum chords in the rhythm indicated. Use the chord diagrams found at the top of the first page of the transcription for the appropriate chord voicings. Round noteheads indicate single notes.

THE MUSICAL STAFF shows pitches and rhythms and is divided by bar lines into measures. Pitches are named after the first seven letters of the alphabet.

TABLATURE graphically represents the guitar fingerboard. Each horizontal line represents a string, and each number represents a fret.

HALF-STEP BEND: Strike the note and bend up 1/2 step.

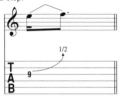

BEND AND RELEASE: Strike the note and bend up as indicated, then release back to the original note. Only the first note is struck.

HAMMER-ON: Strike the first (lower) note with one finger, then sound the higher note (on the same string) with another finger by fretting it without picking.

TRILL: Very rapidly alternate between the notes indicated by continuously hammering on and pulling off.

PICK SCRAPE: The edge of the pick is rubbed down (or up) the string, producing a scratchy sound.

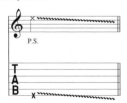

TREMOLO PICKING: The note is picked as rapidly and continuously as possible.

WHOLE-STEP BEND: Strike the note and bend up one step.

PRE-BEND: Bend the note as indicated, then strike it.

PULL-OFF: Place both fingers on the notes to be sounded. Strike the first note and without picking, pull the finger off to sound the second (lower) note.

TAPPING: Hammer ("tap") the fret indicated with the pick-hand index or middle finger and pull off to the note fretted by the fret hand.

MUFFLED STRINGS: A percussive sound is produced by laying the fret hand across the string(s) without depressing, and striking them with the pick hand.

VIBRATO BAR DIVE AND RETURN: The pitch of the note or chord is dropped a specified number of steps (in rhythm), then returned to the original pitch.

GRACE NOTE BEND: Strike the note and immediately bend up as indicated.

VIBRATO: The string is vibrated by rapidly bending and releasing the note with the fretting hand.

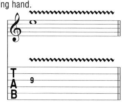

LEGATO SLIDE: Strike the first note and then slide the same fret-hand finger up or down to the second note. The second note is not struck.

NATURAL HARMONIC: Strike the note while the fret-hand lightly touches the string directly over the fret indicated.

PALM MUTING: The note is partially muted by the pick hand lightly touching the string(s) just before the bridge.

VIBRATO BAR SCOOP: Depress the bar just before striking the note, then quickly release the bar.

SLIGHT (MICROTONE) BEND: Strike the note and bend up 1/4 step.

WIDE VIBRATO: The pitch is varied to a greater degree by vibrating with the fretting hand.

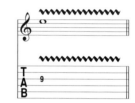

SHIFT SLIDE: Same as legato slide, except the second note is struck.

PINCH HARMONIC: The note is fretted normally and a harmonic is produced by adding the edge of the thumb or the tip of the index finger of the pick hand to the normal pick attack.

RAKE: Drag the pick across the strings indicated with a single motion.

VIBRATO BAR DIP: Strike the note and then immediately drop a specified number of steps, then release back to the original pitch.

GUITAR RECORDED VERSIONS®

Guitar Recorded Versions® are note-for-note transcriptions of guitar music taken directly off recordings. This series, one of the most popular in print today, features some of the greatest guitar players and groups from blues and rock to country and jazz.

Guitar Recorded Versions are transcribed by the best transcribers in the business. Every book contains notes and tablature. Visit www.halleonard.com for our complete selection.

AUTHENTIC TRANSCRIPTIONS
WITH NOTES AND TABLATURE

00690016 The Will Ackerman Collection $19.95	00690829 Boston Guitar Collection $19.99	00690524 Melissa Etheridge – Skin $19.95
00690501 Bryan Adams – Greatest Hits $19.95	00690491 Best of David Bowie.............................$19.95	00690496 Best of Everclear $19.95
00690002 Aerosmith – Big Ones $24.95	00690583 Box Car Racer $19.95	00690515 Extreme II – Pornograffitti $19.95
00692015 Aerosmith – Greatest Hits $22.95	00690873 Breaking Benjamin – Phobia.................$19.95	00690982 Fall Out Boy – Folie à Deux $22.99
00690603 Aerosmith – O Yeah! (Ultimate Hits) $24.95	00690764 Breaking Benjamin – We Are Not Alone $19.95	00690810 Fall Out Boy – From Under the Cork Tree ...$19.95
00690147 Aerosmith – Rocks $19.95	00690451 Jeff Buckley Collection $24.95	00690897 Fall Out Boy – Infinity on High $22.95
00690146 Aerosmith – Toys in the Attic $19.99	00690957 Bullet for My Valentine – Scream Aim Fire ...$19.95	00691009 Five Finger Death Punch $19.99
00690139 Alice in Chains..................................$19.95	00690678 Best of Kenny Burrell $19.95	00690664 Best of Fleetwood Mac.......................$19.95
00690178 Alice in Chains – Acoustic $19.95	00690564 The Calling – Camino Palmero $19.95	00690870 Flyleaf $19.95
00694865 Alice in Chains – Dirt $19.95	00690261 Carter Family Collection $19.95	00690257 John Fogerty – Blue Moon Swamp $19.95
00660225 Alice in Chains – Facelift $19.95	00690043 Best of Cheap Trick $19.95	00690931 Foo Fighters –
00694925 Alice in Chains – Jar of Flies/Sap $19.95	00690171 Chicago – The Definitive Guitar Collection $22.95	Echoes, Silence, Patience & Grace $19.95
00690387 Alice in Chains – Nothing Safe: Best of the Box $19.95	00691004 Chickenfoot $22.99	00690235 Foo Fighters – The Colour and the Shape ...$19.95
00690899 All That Remains – The Fall of Ideals $19.95	00691011 Chimaira Guitar Collection $24.99	00690808 Foo Fighters – In Your Honor $19.95
00690812 All-American Rejects – Move Along $19.95	00690567 Charlie Christian – The Definitive Collection $19.95	00690595 Foo Fighters – One by One $19.95
00690983 All-American Rejects –	00690590 Eric Clapton – Anthology....................$29.95	00690394 Foo Fighters – There Is Nothing Left to Lose ...$19.95
When the World Comes Down $22.99	00692391 Best of Eric Clapton – 2nd Edition $22.95	00690805 Best of Robben Ford $19.95
00694932 Allman Brothers Band –	00690936 Eric Clapton – Complete Clapton $29.95	00690842 Best of Peter Frampton $19.95
Definitive Collection for Guitar Volume 1.................$24.95	00690074 Eric Clapton – Cream of Clapton $24.95	00690734 Franz Ferdinand $19.95
00694933 Allman Brothers Band –	00690247 Eric Clapton – 461 Ocean Boulevard $19.99	00694920 Best of Free $19.95
Definitive Collection for Guitar Volume 2.................$24.95	00690010 Eric Clapton – From the Cradle.............$19.95	00690222 G3 Live – Joe Satriani, Steve Vai,
00694934 Allman Brothers Band –	00690716 Eric Clapton – Me and Mr. Johnson $19.95	and Eric Johnson.............................$22.95
Definitive Collection for Guitar Volume 3.................$24.95	00694873 Eric Clapton – Timepieces $19.95	00694807 Danny Gatton – 88 Elmira St $19.95
00690958 Duane Allman Guitar Anthology $24.99	00694869 Eric Clapton – Unplugged $22.95	00690438 Genesis Guitar Anthology....................$19.95
00690945 Alter Bridge – Blackbird $22.99	00690415 Clapton Chronicles – Best of Eric Clapton $18.95	00690858 David Gilmour – On an Island $24.95
00690755 Alter Bridge – One Day Remains $19.95	00694896 John Mayall/Eric Clapton – Bluesbreakers $19.95	00690753 Best of Godsmack $19.95
00690571 Trey Anastasio $19.95	00690162 Best of the Clash $19.95	00120167 Godsmack.......................................$19.95
00691013 The Answer – Everyday Demons $19.99	00690828 Coheed & Cambria – Good Apollo I'm	00690848 Godsmack – IV $19.95
00690158 Chet Atkins – Almost Alone $19.95	Burning Star, IV, Vol. 1: From Fear Through	00690338 Goo Goo Dolls – Dizzy Up the Girl $19.95
00694876 Chet Atkins – Contemporary Styles $19.95	the Eyes of Madness $19.95	00690576 Goo Goo Dolls – Gutterflower $19.95
00694878 Chet Atkins – Vintage Fingerstyle $19.95	00690940 Coheed and Cambria – No World for Tomorrow $19.95	00690773 Good Charlotte – Chronicles of Life and Death ...$19.95
00690865 Atreyu – A Deathgrip on Yesterday $19.95	00690494 Coldplay – Parachutes $19.95	00690601 Good Charlotte – The Young and the Hopeless $19.95
00690609 Audioslave $19.95	00690593 Coldplay – A Rush of Blood to the Head $19.95	00690927 Patty Griffin – Children Running Through ...$19.95
00690804 Audioslave – Out of Exile $19.95	00690906 Coldplay – The Singles & B-Sides $24.95	00690591 Patty Griffin – Guitar Collection $19.95
00690884 Audioslave – Revelations $19.95	00690962 Coldplay – Viva La Vida $19.95	00690978 Guns N' Roses – Chinese Democracy $24.99
00690926 Avenged Sevenfold $22.95	00690806 Coldplay – X & Y $19.95	00694854 Buddy Guy – Damn Right, I've Got the Blues $19.95
00690820 Avenged Sevenfold – City of Evil............$24.95	00690555 Best of Collective Soul $19.95	00690697 Best of Jim Hall $19.95
00694918 Randy Bachman Collection $22.95	00690928 Chris Cornell – Carry On $19.95	00690840 Ben Harper – Both Sides of the Gun $19.95
00690366 Bad Company – Original Anthology – Book 1 ....$19.95	00694940 Counting Crows – August & Everything After $19.95	00690987 Ben Harper and Relentless7 –
00690367 Bad Company – Original Anthology – Book 2 ....$19.95	00690405 Counting Crows – This Desert Life $19.95	White Lies for Dark Times $22.99
00690503 Beach Boys – Very Best of......................$19.95	00694840 Cream – Disraeli Gears $19.95	00694798 George Harrison Anthology $19.95
00694929 Beatles: 1962-1966 ....$24.95	00690285 Cream – Those Were the Days..............$17.95	00690778 Hawk Nelson – Letters to the President ...$19.95
00694930 Beatles: 1967-1970 ....$24.95	00690352 Creed – My Own Prison $19.95	00690841 Scott Henderson – Blues Guitar Collection $19.95
00690489 Beatles – 1 ....$24.99	00690551 Creed – Weathered $19.95	00692930 Jimi Hendrix – Are You Experienced? $24.95
00694880 Beatles – Abbey Road $19.95	00690819 Best of Creedence Clearwater Revival $22.95	00692931 Jimi Hendrix – Axis: Bold As Love $22.95
00690110 Beatles – Book 1 (White Album) $19.95	00690648 The Very Best of Jim Croce $19.95	00690304 Jimi Hendrix – Band of Gypsys $24.99
00690111 Beatles – Book 2 (White Album) $19.95	00690572 Steve Cropper – Soul Man $19.95	00690321 Jimi Hendrix – BBC Sessions $22.95
00690902 The Beatles – The Capitol Albums, Volume 1 ....$24.99	00690613 Best of Crosby, Stills & Nash $22.95	00690608 Jimi Hendrix – Blue Wild Angel............$24.95
00694832 Beatles – For Acoustic Guitar $22.99	00690777 Crossfade...$19.95	00694944 Jimi Hendrix – Blues $24.95
00690137 Beatles – A Hard Day's Night $16.95	00699521 The Cure – Greatest Hits $24.95	00692932 Jimi Hendrix – Electric Ladyland $24.95
00690482 Beatles – Let It Be $17.95	00690637 Best of Dick Dale $19.95	00690602 Jimi Hendrix – Smash Hits $24.99
00694891 Beatles – Revolver $19.95	00690941 Dashboard Confessional –	00690017 Jimi Hendrix – Woodstock $24.95
00694914 Beatles – Rubber Soul $19.95	The Shade of Poison Trees $19.95	00690843 H.I.M. – Dark Light $19.95
00694863 Beatles – Sgt. Pepper's Lonely Hearts Club Band.....$19.95	00690892 Daughtry $19.95	00690869 Hinder – Extreme Behavior..................$19.95
00690383 Beatles – Yellow Submarine $19.95	00690822 Best of Alex De Grassi $19.95	00660029 Buddy Holly.....................................$19.95
00690632 Beck – Sea Change $19.95	00690967 Death Cab for Cutie – Narrow Stairs $22.99	00690793 John Lee Hooker Anthology $24.99
00694884 Best of George Benson $19.95	00690289 Best of Deep Purple...........................$17.95	00660169 John Lee Hooker – A Blues Legend $19.95
00692385 Chuck Berry $19.95	00690288 Deep Purple – Machine Head $17.99	00694905 Howlin' Wolf $19.95
00690835 Billy Talent.......................................$19.95	00690784 Best of Def Leppard $19.95	00690692 Very Best of Billy Idol $19.95
00690879 Billy Talent II $19.95	00694831 Derek and the Dominos –	00690688 Incubus – A Crow Left of the Murder $19.95
00690149 Black Sabbath $14.95	Layla & Other Assorted Love Songs $22.95	00690457 Incubus – Make Yourself....................$19.95
00690901 Best of Black Sabbath $19.95	00692240 Bo Diddley – Guitar Solos by Fred Sokolow $19.99	00690544 Incubus – Morningview......................$19.95
00690148 Black Sabbath – Master of Reality...........$14.95	00690384 Best of Ani DiFranco $19.95	00690136 Indigo Girls – 1200 Curfews $22.95
00690142 Black Sabbath – Paranoid $14.95	00690322 Ani DiFranco – Little Plastic Castle $19.95	00690790 Iron Maiden Anthology......................$24.99
00692200 Black Sabbath – We Sold Our	00690380 Ani DiFranco – Up Up Up Up Up Up $19.95	00690887 Iron Maiden – A Matter of Life and Death ...$24.95
Soul for Rock 'N' Roll $19.95	00690979 Best of Dinosaur Jr............................$19.99	00690730 Alan Jackson – Guitar Collection $19.95
00690674 blink-182 ....$19.95	00690833 Private Investigations –	00694938 Elmore James – Master Electric Slide Guitar $19.95
00690389 blink-182 – Enema of the State $19.95	Best of Dire Straits and Mark Knopfler $24.95	00690652 Best of Jane's Addiction $19.95
00690831 blink-182 – Greatest Hits $19.95	00695382 Very Best of Dire Straits – Sultans of Swing $19.95	00690721 Jet – Get Born $19.95
00690523 blink-182 – Take Off Your Pants and Jacket $19.95	00690347 The Doors – Anthology.......................$22.95	00690684 Jethro Tull – Aqualung $19.95
00690028 Blue Oyster Cult – Cult Classics $19.95	00690348 The Doors – Essential Guitar Collection ...$16.95	00690693 Jethro Tull Guitar Anthology $19.95
00690851 James Blunt – Back to Bedlam $22.95	00690915 Dragonforce – Inhuman Rampage $29.99	00690647 Best of Jewel $19.95
00690008 Bon Jovi – Cross Road $19.95	00690250 Best of Duane Eddy $16.95	00698898 John 5 – The Devil Knows My Name $22.95
00690827 Bon Jovi – Have a Nice Day $22.95	00690533 Electric Light Orchestra Guitar Collection $19.95	00690959 John 5 – Requiem $22.95
00690913 Boston $19.95	00690909 Best of Tommy Emmanuel $19.95	00690814 John 5 – Songs for Sanity $19.95
00690932 Boston – Don't Look Back $19.99	00690555 Best of Melissa Etheridge.....................$19.95	00690751 John 5 – Vertigo $19.95

AUTHENTIC TRANSCRIPTIONS WITH NOTES AND TABLATURE

FOR MORE INFORMATION, SEE YOUR LOCAL MUSIC DEALER,
OR WRITE TO:

HAL•LEONARD®
CORPORATION

7777 W. BLUEMOUND RD. P.O. BOX 13819 MILWAUKEE, WI 53213

Complete songlists and more at www.halleonard.com
Prices, contents, and availability subject to change without notice.

0110